Sounds
That
A r o u s e
me

*Bern Porter
at Colby April 9, 1993*

Also by Bern Porter

Doldrums: A Study in Surrealism, 1941
Waterfight, 1941
Art Techniques, 1947
Drawings: 1955-56, 1957
Physics for Tomorrow, 1959
Scandinavian Summer: A Psycho-Visual Recollection, 1961
Aphasia: A Psycho-Visual Satire, 1961
I've Left, 1963
What Henry Miller Said and Why It Is Important, 1964
Art Productions: 1928-1965, 1965
468B :Thy Future, 1966
Dieresis, 1969
Knox County, Maine, A Regional Report, 1969
The Manhattan Telephone Book, 1972
Wastemaker: 1926-1961, 1972
Found Poems, 1972
Where To Go, What To do When In New York, 1974
Selected Founds, 1975
Run-On, 1975
Gee-Whizzels, 1977
American Strange, 1978
Isla Vista, 1981
The Book of Do's, 1982
Here Comes Everybody's Don't Book, 1984
My My Dear Me, 1985
The Last Acts of Saint Fuckyou, 1985
Horizontal Hold, 1985
Neverends, 1988
Sweet End, 1989
The Book of Light, 1990
Vocrescends, 1990
CRCNCL, 1991
Numbers, 1991

Bibliographies by Bern Porter

Henry Miller: A Chronology and Bibliography, 1945
H. L. Mencken, A Bibliography, 1957
The First Publications of F. Scott Fitzgerald, 1960
Wernher von Braun, 1965

Biographies (about Bern Porter)

The Roaring Market and the Silent Tomb, James Schevill, 1957
Where to Go, What to Do, When You Are Bern Porter: A Personal Biography, James Schevill, Tilbury House, 1992

Edited and with an
introduction
by Mark Melnicove

Sounds

That

Selected
Writings

Arouse

me

Bern Porter

Tilbury House, Publishers
Gardiner, Maine

to scholars Janelle
and Anna

Tilbury House, Publishers
132 Water Street
Gardiner, ME 04345

First Printing

Library of Congress Cataloging-in-Publication Data

Porter, Bern, 1911-
    Sounds that arouse me : selected writings / Bern Porter :
edited and with an introduction by Mark Melnicove.
        p.   cm.
    Includes bibliographical references.
    ISBN 0-88448-101-8 (pbk.) : $9.95
    I. Melnicove, Mark. II. Title.
PS3566.06299A6   1992
700' .92--dc20   92-31861
                                                      CIP

10 9 8 7 6 5 4 3 2 1

Contents

Introduction

The first time I saw Bern Porter he was slumped in a chair, head cradled in his hands, absorbed in thought. Periodically, he'd run his fingers, in lieu of a comb, through his wavy gray hair. But nothing, not even that self-massaging, seemed to satisfy him; there was an air of irritability about him, as if he would welcome the chance to stand up and kick someone in the teeth.

We were present at a nuts-and-bolts session on small press publishing at the 1978 Maine Poets Festival, held at the College of the Atlantic in Bar Harbor, Maine. The meeting room overlooked the sparkling waters of Frenchman's Bay, yet Porter, off in a corner by himself, looked grief-stricken, as if that were no mere skull in his possession, but the world in all its turmoil. As he sat there snorting and grunting, he looked like a man who had, in his youth, invented the twentieth century, but now in his twilight years was dismayed to see that it wasn't turning out as expected.

> Porter could get elected to the Irony Hall of Fame, special joke's-on-you division. When he went to Hiroshima after the war to stand at the epicenter and grieve, he found people there selling souvenirs.
> C. Carr, "A Little Spin Through the Cul-de-Sac: Bern Porter's Quantum Leaps," The Village Voice, October 9, 1984.

As a young physicist in his early thirties, Porter was drafted to work on the development of the atom bomb, one of thousands employed by the top-secret Manhattan Project. Security was so tight that only a select few (Porter not among them) knew the true nature of the project's mission. Like any other citizen, Porter learned the horrible news of August 6, 1945, through the mass media (in his case *The New York Times*). As he wrote in "Growing Up in the Nuclear Age" (p. 128), he "read not only that a bomb had been dropped on Hiroshima, but also exactly what I had been doing with my life and talents the past four years at Princeton [where he met Einstein], Oak Ridge [where he supervised the separation of uranium into its isotopes at a plant on the Clinch River], Berkeley [where he worked at the Lawrence Radiation Laboratory]. . . ."

In 1944, [Porter] published [Henry] Miller's anti-war tract,

Murder the Murderer, which did not endear him to the United States government. Shortly after that,—in spite of the general popularity of the war effort (difficult for us, in the aftermath of Korea, Lebanon, Vietnam and Cambodia to imagine),—Porter quit [the Manhattan Project], an act of incredible courage. He was not about to contribute to the extermination of the civilians of Hiroshima and Nagasaki. This was done in typical Porter style—no fanfare, no news releases: just the action, to speak for itself. Like his works.
Dick Higgins, introduction to Porter's I've Left, Something Else Press, New York, 1971.

The atom bomb that destroyed Hiroshima blasted a hole through Porter's idealism. The memory still dogs him, an ever-deepening wound that no amount of repentance can mend (*I want to run but have nowhere to go*—"Days in the Early Eighties," page 140). It created a split between the artist and scientist in him that he has been trying to reconcile ever since. His book *I've Left* (first published in 1963 by the Marathon Press, Pasadena, California, and reissued in 1971 by Dick Higgins's Something Else Press) is a prophetic vision of the union of science and art, a testament to the struggle within his soul to integrate the transcendent qualities of the creative act with the potential for harmony with nature as represented by science. That science is used for destructive purposes brings tears to his eyes every time he talks about it. It should come as no surprise that Porter, while living on Guam in the early 1950s, began to look toward tribal cultures for solutions to our modern dilemmas.

born on valentine day 1911. from 1918 to 1922 bern's father brot home every week a sunday paper publisht by hearst. if a newspaper is literature and he believes it is, at the age of 9 this was the only literature he saw, he read every word and became aware that his understanding didnt impede his visual enjoyment, his visual excitement. he began to understand visually thru his eyes; it didn't matter what they meant, the words were exciting, and he would cut them out to paste into a scrapbook. (for those who like economical deterministic accents, as a child and young adult bern never had much money. his childhood was spent in poverty. as such his attempt to learn how to see and to be stirred by seeing was done with little expenditure of money).
karl kempton, "One Continuous Exploration Thru the Eye," Kaldron, Issue no.11, Summer 1980.

That day in Bar Harbor, newly arrived in Maine, I had no idea who

Bern Porter was or what he had accomplished. I was not familiar with the key role he had played in San Francisco's post World War II literary renaissance as co-editor of *Circle* magazine and publisher of books by Henry Miller, Kenneth Patchen, Robert Duncan, Philip Lamantia and others. I didn't know that in his twenties he had helped to invent television but was now distraught at its use as a mass opiate; I didn't know he had worked with Von Braun on the Saturn moon rocket in Huntsville, Alabama, writing at the time (1965) in a letter to the Maine Author Collection at the Maine State Library, "We're assembled now in this place [Huntsville], getting ready to go to the moon! Could it be because we have made a mess of the earth?"; I didn't know that he was an originator of what have come to be called artists books, his first creations as an nine-year old in Houlton, Maine, being bartered for eggs and other essentials; I didn't know that he was an ardent admirer of Wilhelm Reich and had for years been trying in the cellar of his house in Belfast to replicate Reich's results with orgone energy, only to have years of careful experimentation wiped out when a neighbor clearcut his woods, diverting an underground stream and flooding Porter's cellar; I didn't know his second wife, Margaret, to whom Porter had been married for twenty years, had died three years earlier in 1975, a loss that Porter would never get over, a grief that would always emanate from him like the tarnished albedo of a broken moon. As I stood off to the side, watching him that first time, Porter would sometimes butt into the festival's proceedings, like a geyser going off unpredictably, contradicting everything that had preceded, then return to his statuesque thinking/bemoaning pose in the chair. He answered even the most straightforward, technical queries with information that was often inaccurate and misleading. If he wanted to give the appearance of being a crackpot, he was doing an excellent job of it.

> You've given me books in the past and also more encouragement probably than you realised from long time back by your own presence and sincere activity on West Coast continuing the old tradition of independent printing of individual American-grain solitary Muse which was a tradition I'd always aspired to be part of.
> *Allen Ginsberg, in a letter to Bern Porter.*

Later that night, I saw Porter shine, free of psychic baggage. He performed a stand-up, improvisational "rendering" (as he called it) of non-literary texts that were handed to him, sight unseen, by members of the festival audience. His method of reading, chanting, and mumbling the words, phrases, syllables, and phonemes of credit cards, matchbook covers, and the like was spellbinding and often hilarious. He displayed a mastery of dead-pan invective, parody, and irony. While he was performing, his partner, musician Charlie Morrow, accompanied him by percussively brushing Porter's body and clothes with a hairbrush. The next day I bought a copy of each of Porter's books of found poetry, most of them self-published, that he sold for $2 a piece at a table that he manned himself. He replaced the copies I bought with fresh ones from a small suitcase decorated with labels from Greyhound bus trips he had recently taken. (Porter doesn't have a driver's license; doesn't own a car—see "Are Automobiles Necessary?," page 146.) When I returned home and showed Porter's books to my literal-minded friends, they thought I was crazy. What's so great about these, they asked? Anyone can cut up newspapers and magazines and make art; what a waste of money, they intoned.

> Some of the found poetry of Bern Porter is like this—you can open a book and see things there that look like poems, but they're laundry lists, or they're cut up bits of ads, or pages of mail order catalogues. Whatever. But in some way they become poems too, particularly, say, the way a really good found-poet like Bern Porter utilizes them.
> Jerome Rothenberg, "Changing the Present, Changing the Past: A New Poetics," in Talking Poetics from Naropa Institute: Annals of the Jack Kerouac School of Disembodied Poetics, Volume Two, Shambhala, Boulder and London, 1979, page 260.

When we first met I was 26; he was 67, old enough to be my father. I was just starting out as a publisher; the books he had designed and published on a shoestring were beautiful and inspirational. I was experimenting with alternatives to straight readings of my poems; the performances he gave showed me ways to explore the full range of my voice. I was making visual poems; the hundreds of pages he had produced with their innumerable typesizes and varied typographies seduced me to create poems that would engage all the senses, not just the eyes. The chemistry between us was not to be denied.

We began to perform our poetry together, touring Maine and the Northeast wherever or whenever we were invited. I cooked him meals; I drove him to signings, openings, happenings and performances; I published his books; I listened to his stories; together we discussed and laughed about everything that had to do with art, literature, culture, and romance. During those early years in our relationship, Bern was in the midst of a painful and disillusioning divorce from his third wife; some of the poems in this book (Section IV) date from that period and are among his best. As we traveled, performed, and got to know each other Bern never said we must do this, you must do that, this would be better than that, etc. His only injunction was that no matter what we intoned, chanted, recited, or danced, no matter how we lived, it must be "spontaneous and unrehearsed."

> "The old thing is over" according to Mr. Porter—the old thing being thousands of years of increasingly deprived senses, of consciousness limping along in the unfortunate vehicles of conventional language, texts, plays and one-dimensional narrative structures. Referring to himself as a "plasma of energy," Bern Porter quietly insists that his work involves the tapping of the entire range of human sensual possibility—an enterprise that will require "200 years because of the lapsed condition of our sensory awareness."
> Bud Navero, "Bern Porter's Sci/Art," Soho News Weekly, January, 18-24, 1979.

Many of the writings in this book have been kept almost secret. Porter has been so insistent ("Song," page 32) that we "skip the meaning, find the spirit, the soul, essential essence, the meat thereof (especially the meat, brother)" that he has tended to undervalue his works where meaning and narration *is* essential and not push for their publication (except for the avalanche of letters to the editor he sends to the two newspapers in his hometown of Belfast—see page 13). Some of these writings, such as "All Over The Place" (page 35), "Statement" (page 42), and "How It Works in ABC Form" (page 45), contain the theoretical underpinnings of his found poems and sculpture, performance pieces, and artists books. Some come from observations gleaned during ocean cruises he has taken over the past 15 years; the first cruise financed, in part, by a creative writing fellowship grant from the National Endowment for the Arts, the rest by wealthy Chicago patron Marion C. Gettleman. Still others come from interviews with him published in little magazines and by small presses (including *Bern! Porter! Interview!*, the first book of his that I published).

The way in which Porter admires Henry Miller ("Henry Miller," p. 85) could also describe himself: "He's the only person I've ever met whose written words are the exact duplicate of his spoken words. . . . When he speaks it's like a torrent, like a waterfall, and there's no stopping him, no shutting him off. Fantastic imagery, word flow. And he writes the same way."

> The last time I saw Bern Porter, he was returning his attention to the wheel. "It's been greatly misunderstood, and used

rather poorly," he suggested.
Tom Bryan, publisher of "Not Famous Enough Americans" maple syrup labels of which No. 2, in 1984, profiled the life and work of Bern Porter.

Like all innovators, Porter is obsessed with his work. And yet, in spite of all that seriousness, the man's sense of humor and irony is superbly quick-witted. His writings and other works suggest that the only way to get a handle on contemporary culture, as demented and bruised as it has become, is through satire. But Porter is no slap-dash cynic; he is reverent where it counts, in matters of the heart and earth. *Sounds That Arouse Me* ends with his theories about plasma and the membrane that separates life from death, ignorance from knowledge. Neither easy to know, nor gentle in his prophecy, Porter insists that we open up all the senses (there are more than just five) and "VOICE THE ESSENCE, BLOW THE THING, PUSH IT HIGH, WIDE, DEEP, AND HANDSOME" ("Song," page 33). It is an eternal message that will live beyond his years.

Mark Melnicove
Gardiner, Maine
August 1992

1

I sincerely hope you have
a good memory for faces
because there is no mirror
in the house.

The Packages

The sugar is packaged
The salt is packaged
The pepper is packaged
The bread is packaged
The biscuits are packaged
The cookies are packaged
The jelly is packaged
The relish is packaged
The sauce is packaged
The ketchup is packaged
The books are packaged
The newspapers are packaged
The coffee is packaged
The tea is packaged
The milk is packaged
The fork is packaged
The spoons are packaged
The toothpicks are packaged
The tumbler is packaged
The toilet seat is packaged
The cup is packaged
The mayonnaise is packaged
The blanket is packaged
     I am packaged
     Pray tell
     How can I ever
        open **myself?**

I am male. I wear standard male clothes. That is to say my clothes are exactly like the clothing of every other male. This morning fresh from the shower I stepped into a pair of shorts and drew them to their proper height while buttoning the lower button. I pulled over my head the standard sleeveless undershirt, tucked it under my shorts and buttoned the top two buttons. Men who are smarter than I am put the shirt on first and draw the shorts up over it. Note that now I probably have on all that propriety demands: shorts and shirt. Note that I have two layers of cloth about my waist, but only one layer about my legs and chest. Note that I have used three buttons or equivalent snap-ons. I have gone through nine separate motions to get into this state. And now notice that as I continue dressing I will merely be donning an elongated version of what I already wear.

I pull on my trousers, draw on and tuck down a dress shirt, making a total of four layers of cloth about my waist with only one layer on my arms and legs. The adjustment of trousers' front and belt after getting them on consumes in all eight separate motions. Then follows the folding of the cuffs and insertion of links, the placement and adjustment of arm bands. The collar is next with buttons or equivalents front and back plus the necktie, a finicky kind of operation which allows males to primp and preen at their best.

At this point I have seven pockets. I have used thirteen buttons. I have gone through forty-one separate motions. I am at last ready to put a fifth layer of cloth about my waist in the form of a vest. It has four pockets on the outside with one secret pocket for supposedly secret purposes on the inside. This vest has five more buttons and requires six more body movements with possibly the adjustment of a strap and buckle arrangement in the back needing five more movements.

I am now ready for my suit, that is to say I am ready for the sixth layer of cloth about my waist. I am ready for three more buttons and four more pockets. This I accomplish with six body movements followed with a final adjustment of the ensemble which includes the insertion of a billfold, watch and two handkerchiefs in four of the seventeen pockets now available to me. Straightening again the tie and collar brings the total up to sixty-seven movements, not including of course the shoes, socks, and garters I had put on soon after my trousers were in place and with twelve exacting motions.

Note that I am now ready for the wars of survival as we know them . . . in short I am dressed. Note that I have on eleven separate garments or items. Note that these items have twenty-eight appurtenances. Note that only my legs are now covered with a single layer of cloth, that is my legs five inches above and five inches below my kneecaps. Notice that fourteen buttons have been used, two shoe laces, two cuf links, two arm bands, one belt, one tie clasp, two collar buttons and one necktie, plus one zipper, two garters and seven buttonholes which are not really buttonholes but only imitations of them. For some unaccountable reason six of these false buttonholes have buttons but the seventh does not.

Obviously I am now neither scientifically, logically nor functionally and aesthetically dressed. And I have expended a quarter of a million movements in the thirty-six thousand times I have dressed myself these past forty years. Moreover the way out of this unfortunate tradition and profits bound dilemma is both obscure and difficult.

I begin by combining. A vest and shirt in one piece. A combine of these two with the undershirt. Then adding the coat or jacket for a four-in-one unit, the whole without pockets, arm bands, cufflinks, collars, buttons, collar buttons. I combine the trousers with the undershorts, dropping in the process cuffs, one belt, three pockets and all buttons. I am seeking a single-piece affair with the necktie, the most useless of all useless apparel and yet the one object of greatest affection and most difficult to part with, being the last to go.

My first one-piece, all-occasion suit, not including stockings and shoes, has no cuffs, collar, tie, belt, double thickness at any point, and only three pockets. The requirements of porosity, flexibility, freedom of movement, warmth and low production costs plus functional styling necessitate considerable research with materials ending in the creation of woven paper, glass and tin textiles each made from the commonly wasted by-products of civilization: glass bottles, tin cans and waste paper of all sorts. Woven plastic, cellophane, cork, linoleum, and wood are also tried along with many natural reeds and fibers growing neglected and unused in great abundance throughout the world. Coupled with this search of mine for materials is the first study ever made of the engineering structure and design of the body and analysis of its movements and functions, the better to design the first garment ever conceived from these obvious viewpoints. Interestingly enough the ultimate suit is a coated or sprayed on type which is removed instantly by dissolving, with reapplication as frequently as desired. Any wanted thickness and color or combinations of color are of course possible. An intermediate or somewhat popular model of my design having built-in soles or shoes is dispensed from slot machines and is disposable in toilets.

7

Similarly I investigate wear spots on seats, elbows, garment edges subject to handling and wear. Methods of keeping materials perpetually clean and soil proof and permanently preserved are equally examined. It is while comparing the stylization potential of American-made shoes with the ready functionalism of a Japanese sandal that I attack the weardown features of heels and toes and the wearout characteristic of leather soles. Side tracking the complaints of the highly organized shoe repair industry and the shoe and hide producers who are always pleased to have shoes deteriorate rapidly, I set up motion picture cameras of varying speeds on busy street corners in the first known attempt to learn how people walk and just what strains are produced, at what points and how to correct them either by a change of walking gait or by reshaping the footwear itself. Thus I make thousands of stress, strain and motion studies, I carefully investigate thousands of materials.

As the work goes on in this controlled and investigative manner I foresee that human skin can never be improved upon, might under the right conditions be made to grow to suit better a given purpose. Thus by special vitamin injections into skin structures in the soles of human feet I develop there a heavier, tougher skin which takes all conditions of use without the need of additional protection or covering. The human foot for the first time in history is taken for what it already is, a thing of great beauty, great functionalism. Unadorned feet at last come into their own. The only problem is to teach people to use them so that their natural beauty can evince itself. The same is true of all body parts and coverings which I develop. Skin alone is superior, cannot be excelled. These exhaustive studies produce then ways and means of making and being the body beautiful: how to stand, sit, walk or run. More important how to supply, reserve and build it in natural conformity to its true self.

The effect of my work is to change radically whole segments of existing industry. Clothing as we know it today is no longer made; unemployed garment workers become teachers of the body beautiful. The once shoe manufacturers make devices of leather for rubbing and exercising the body. Cleaning and dyeing establishments, weaving and carding mills are taken over by huge new cosmetic industries now having an entire body to cover with oils, perfumes, paints and preparations of the trade once limited to heads and hands. In fact as the work advances the sprayed-on coverings of my early design, the disposable one-piece suits, the shoes with high-heat treated spring steel soles, the suits with the wearout-proof seats and elbows, the master special that has no pockets but carries all necessary extras pinned on, the mothproof, fadeproof material whose weave and color design changes by simple exposure to ultra-violet light, these and a staggering number of innovations for clothes coming from my personal studio are made obsolete by the simple discovery that the human body without embellishment is superior to anything that can be prepared. The contribution of this great and thoroughly tested truth to the proper areas of the world's population who currently practice it in part, but need further experimental confirmation, is of course tremendous. It only remains now to see that this body is properly fed, rested, exercised and made disease-proof.

8

Industrious, seething ants, those bundles of nervous activity that symbolize a fertile brain, slouch exhausted in their tracks. Some die.

Others, like leaves from those trees that daily grow in the mind as expanding ideas, plume off onto the hard brain floor, leaving puny listless branches drooping indolently.

Arid breezes that lightly trip across the barren wastes of the mind—lapping waves that play upon the sandy shores of the brain's far recesses—stagnate.

No self-motivated ideas or lumbering vehicles of communication pass through that formerly well-travelled way: only dull silence remains suspended and motionless within the cranial void.

The material body naps.

Swinging periodically between unconsciousness
and awareness, the mind, meanwhile, agitates nubilous gases below
the cerebrum, forcing vapors through a fissure in the brain floor.
Languidly, they dance and curl slowly into alphabetical shapes.
Without warning the letters suddenly rearrange themselves into:

D
    O
          S
   O   **E** **M**   **T**
H   **I**   **N**
     G!

a cryptic message whose metallic ring resounds loudly through the
long winding corridors of the skull.

The physical body awakens with a start.

"DO SOMETHING!" echoes the call, crystal clear.

From out of the reddish haze that tints the sky over the
fetid pool come the confused sounds of things done or being done:
pounding typewriters. . .turning wheels . . . riveting hammers..and
driving engines.

"AMOUNT TO SOMETHING," urge the
gaseous letters.

"Write a book and confound the critics; paint an
unintelligible picture and please the aesthetes.

Build a bridge and collect the tolls; loan the filthy
money and count the interest.

Compose a talking couplet, design a ten-way

switch; instigate a revolution, reorganize the nation!

"DO SOMETHING!"

Three red ants stir under the impact, rise halfheart-edly, then collapse into total inactivity.

A tree leaf rustles on the stone plateau as the breeze tries to bestir. Lethargic, it too dies and the leaf wilts.

The material body turns over.

Only the soft, futile nothingness of sleep prevails.

The
Westfield

God gave me a gift
My Grandma laid it
on the radio
I lost it

So say the handwritten words on the walls of an eight by
eight bedroom of the Westfield where
> there is no soap
> two light bulbs won't light
> the ceiling is collapsing
> the bureau is broken
> the chair is broken
> the nightstand is broken
> no coat hangers
> no rug
> no waste basket
> a torn window curtain
> > held closed by a safety pin

Only a white sink
Two sheets and a pillow case on a questionable **bed.**

Dear Independent:

It is hoped the city budget people consider the following Belfast constituents:

1. The In and Outers. Those who work here but can't afford sewer rates, water rates, tax rates so they come in the morning and go out at night.

2. The Nest-Eggers. Those who saved a nest egg for old age and find themselves broke by the 20th of the month.

3. The Inflatees. Those who can't reach up to Jaret & Cohn price levels and so can't live here anymore.

4. The Retirees. Those who do not go out after 6 p.m. because of wild youths, the drug scene and fear of being eaten by dogs.

5. The No Increasees. Those who did not get a salary increase three years ago, two years ago, last year, this year nor will they in any future year.

6. The No Fifty-Centers. Those who never heard of such an increase and never ever received it, nor ever will.

7. The Sayer-Like-It-Isers. Those who insist the city, the county, the schools overmilked the public teat in 1987.

8. The No County Guys and Gals. Those who feel county government should have vanished 20 years ago.

9. The Hydrant Pluggers. Those who reject $80,000 rent and want water meters on every hydrant to be read only if and when water is used.

10. The No Wasters. Those who object to waste in magazine subscriptions, oversanding on city streets, advertising for librarians when they are already at work and the general waste that goes on daily.

11. The Three Layer-Payers. Those who are long overburdened with paying state police, county police, city police.

12. The No Foreigner Crowd. Those who bless the by-pass every day and don't want anyone coming in to increase taxes.

13. The Non-Unionists. Those who do not and will not recognize unions, would require taxpayer permission to negotiate with them and do not recognize settlements nor pay them and remind city hall that settlements over $50,000 require taxpayer permission. No such permission has been or is granted and thus are illegal.

14. The Readers. Those who want a new sidewalk at the library, more books off the floors and a water meter off their ribs.

15. That Culture Bunch. Those who after years of effort finally want the official public blessing of the city administration, the business, the professional and the social community of Belfast for *all* cultural events.

16. The Wharfers. Those who want the piles sticking up off Diamond Park to have something useful on top and the burnt piles and staging removed.

17. The Hotelers. Those who want the unused potato factory at Diamond Park made into a hotel.

18. The Muralists. Those who want all large public wall space painted with murals by local artists.

19. Those Festival People. Tired of the old chicken thing they want many new equivalents and more often.

20. The Pendleton Streeters. Who want the activity to increase there and the junk heap at the lower end zoned out.

21. The Free Helper/Volunteer Set. Who want their presence and willingness more widely known.

22. Le Politic Generale. All of us, including those who make budgets.

15

Jesus Wants Me For A Sunbeam

I

Now that Classic Coke
      is back
And Old Coke and New Coke
      have gone
And fresh horse meat
      is scarce
I've taken to eating cob
      webs for their high
      protein content
And the slipping feeling
      they give my gullet
      as they go down

II

Now that Nancy Reagan
      is in charge
And both Mamie and Beth
      have gone
And hairpins are quite passé
I've taken to playing polo
      for its horsey risk
And the fun of falling off
      as I charge about

III

Now that the price of silver
      has dropped

And the dollar is falling fast
And McDonald's has hit
    four billion
I've taken to painting
    chairs a very pale
       green
Thinking I'm making a
    contribution to **husbandry**

How Many Sons Do You Have?

It was not, definitely not, where you from?
How many times you been here?
What deck you on?
You have stocks, bonds, yes?
You speak English?
Your name, please.
What country you like?
You drive a Mercedes, no?
Was your aunt ever in Egypt?
What's your politics?
Ever in Malta?
Of course you've read Herman Hesse?
Did you see Pickle Fever?
Been in Lisbon?
Like Rock?
What church you go to?
What's your drink?
Which food do you like the best?
But simply
How many sons do you have?
(And with the understanding of course that if you have six
he has seven.)
Like if you say you've been
On the ship less than eleven times
Or been around the world less than fourteen times
You are a no class, creditless slob
So on the son thing
You say nothing.
Because not having any
Or the prospects of getting one/any
It's the simple truth
You never had any sons

19

Do not now have sons
And by implication
You have had no love affairs
Have no wife
No chance at love affairs
Daughters either for that matter
And hence are not a man.
No **sons.**

The Cold
Fish Saga

When Mother said
I was a cold fish
She did not specify
Cod
Halibut
Trout
Sword
Or
Finnan Haddie
All cold.
She only called me
A Cold Fish.
To which I reply
Yes, I am cold
In temperature
In mannerisms
In approaches
In techniques
In ways generale
But being a fish
That I do not know.
As a matter of fact
I do not know
Much about fish.
When people ask me
If I go fishing
I always say
Yes I do. I
Go down to the
Fish Isle at
The Super Market
And debate for

A very long time
Whether I'll
Take Norwegian
Alaskan, Swedish
Or Maine Sardines.
Which ones are
The cheapest
I always ask
And as I leave
The Fish Isle
At the Super Market
I'm embarrassed
That the cheapest
Sardines the
Ones I've bought
Are not from the
State of Maine.
Another traitor
Some would say
Or as my mother
Says a traitor fish
But are
Sardines really
Fish or
Approximate
Imitation fish?
I don't think they
Count as fish
And furthermore
I am not
One of those
Certainly not
And not that **cold.**

Song
Titles

Your tiny beautiful hand is cold: please be very careful
where you put it

Please don't be mad at yourself if you are now not as
cute as you were when you were three months old

I sincerely hope you have a good memory for faces because
there is no mirror in the house

Pray don't berate your mother unduly, she didn't like
your father either

If the public telephone on the wall does not do what you
want it to do, do not get mad and punch it

Should the noises of small children annoy you don't
shout and scream at them simply blow your nose
twice and throw a shoe

I always go to bed at night with my clothes on so I
won't have to dress myself in the morning

When we got rich my husband had my teeth capped to
reduce the cluck cluck sounds of my eating but then I
had trouble eating corn on the cob

My husband always called me Mother mainly because
he was twenty-three years older than I was

A poor husband is better than no husband, a condition
I would know, having had three of them, one rich,
one poor and one not at all

Why don't you call me up sometime for a chat—preferably
when you are reasonably certain I am not at home

Barbara's Belfast

Lacking ten distinct pieces of silverware
Or even three sizes of spoons
And no three sizes or kinds of knives
And two sizes of forks—
As a matter of fact
With only one each
Of knife, fork and spoon
Barbara's Belfast
Still rates high
In the culinary restaurante arts
Of food and drink
Local style that is.
To be sure there are no tablecloths
Only paper place mats
On Tuesdays
Advertising beer
And no flowers, fresh or dried
No pepper grinders
Silver sugar bowls
Saucers, doilies for iced tea in glasses
A disk of lemon wedges running over
A tray of iced hors d'oeuvres
Just laundered blue cloth napkins
Nor blue and red upholstered chairs
With uniformed boys to push them
In place when one sits down
Or withdraw when one rises to leave
One seats/unseats himself in fact
In a well used chair
Up to or from a well used table
Which doesn't seat five
But only two

Three if crowded which it rarely is.
The menu?
Is it printed for morning breakfasts
On an attractive seven by twelve inch card
With nine subdivisions:

23

     Chilled Juices
     Fruits
     Cereals Hot or Cold
     Eggs
     Meat
     Omelets
     Hot Cakes
     Bread
     Beverages
     With a daily special
     "Our chef de cuisine recommends say
     Cream Mushrooms on Toast"
     For Wednesdays?
Obviously not
And is there one changed daily for the evening meal
With spaces filled over two large pages
Of hand set type, correctly annotated
For fifteen subdivisions in all:

     To Stimulate Your Palate
     From the Tureens
     Our Seafood Tonight
     From Our Italian Cuisine
     Entree Selection
     Vegetables
     Potatoes
     From the Garden
     Your Choice of Dressing
     Low Calorie Platter
     Compotes
     Cheeses
     From Our Pastry Chef
     Fruit
     Beverages

    & Specially ordered wine
      by the half bottle?

24

Most definitely not.
For whatever they have
And whatever you want
Is hand chalked in white on a 3 by 3 blackboard
With what's already sold marked out
So get in early
Say 10:55 and no later for lunch at noon
And for night time dinner don't come at all
Because there isn't **any.**

25

Belfast, ME,
March 14,
1979

Spangled
     treads
The drifting octaves
           below
Sift the interval of lost hours
To dance

This sparse winter we've run a southern line
in opulence with gown, shawls, topaz and diamonds
as if they were always so knowing full well it
is not but nearing near the last

No more greats
None with carpeted stair
The long corridors
Heavy meals
Light wines
        in crystal
A fresh plate with
   every succulent course

This dream

Together we joist the dancers, brush wide
the floor in dangle and shake

It is the future we **know**

Limpid running water flows profusely over the fabric's surface. Hesitating momentarily, it settles vehemently inward, seeking to wet. Deep, damp, deeper and more moist the penetrating water soaks.

Contrarily, the little arid threads quail, though sporadically and undaunted, they soon recover. Mustering all resistance, they stiffen resolutely in defiance, girding themselves individually and collectively against the oncoming flow.

"Check water with water!" the fibers cry, groping excitedly, hastily forcing the scant supply within themselves up to the surface.

"Check water with dams!" they argue, inhaling spasmodically and forming constrictions throughout their entire length.

"Fight the water!"

"Resist the dampness!"

"Check the stream!"

"Fight!"

But humid and damp continues the flow. Down, around, in and throughout the water surges, expecting to moisten, sop and wet.

Quickly, a parched thread is surrounded. This indolent bit of cotton, surreptitiously embedded among the woolens, is cruelly tantalized. Then, charitably, the water appeases her thirst.

Thus abetted, the scheming fiend reverses his tactics. Forcing into the thread, he drenches, chokes and fully saturates it. Damp and wet, the foolhardy one succumbs.

"Stop the water . . .

Oppose that flow . . .

Resist!" cry other arid members. Without heeding, the water surrounds and fills them completely.

"Stop."

"Stop the flow."

"Cut the . . ."

Onward, outward spreads the stream . . . its pliant body, dividing and trickling through the cotton masses, gains pressure. Soon, brute force, forays the remaining, oil-armoured threads of wool. The water vaporizes into surrounding air; lays a damp curtain for the attack. Penetrating, it gushes and swells—deeply undermining and sopping as it moves.

"Stop!"

"Fi . . ."

One surge. One full sweep of the slowly gathered force and water closes inward from all directions . . .

The bruised arteries of the stifled woolen skeins inflate under the growing compression of an aqueous pincer . . .

At the point of bursting, their whole diameter throbs with the coursing flow . . .

The spaces between them are glutted with moisture.

By now all the threads feel cold and damp.

The fabric is wet.

All wet

!

Not At All:
A Psalm Written
In Tumultuous Days

29

Bear
Mountain, NY,
1943

Oh praise non-existence: laud the prevalence of nothing, every-body.

Endorse naught, popularize its name; believe therein day after day.

Spread its doctrine among riders, self-movers and anyone stationary; induce non-supporters to say aye.

For nothing begets not a thing: neither anything at all, nor aught whatever arises from it.

Personal exertion and sacrifice for the sake of worthlessness are unknown; so too are collusion, violation, acquisition and destruction.

Extol nonentity, all wearers of slogans: give not at all its just pedestal.

Bring pencil and paper for note-taking, put a little something in the slot and interpret the ensuing silence.

Explain to onlookers that nothing excels: zero does not promote poverty, disorder and International War.

Let the networks elucidate, the stage and screen drama-
tize; let the air resound and the vast extent thereof.

30

Let nothing permeate the land and all that are therein;
then shall everyone live quietly together.

For it in nowise bestirs: neither something nor anything
at all is produced, nothing that is except useful quiet-useful to the
non-existing.

2

I am saying, then, that there
is no reason why the
subject matter of art and
the methods of its presenta-
tion should remain forever
unchanged.

Song

32

Belfast, ME,
1977

Sing now
Evenly voiced
The sound beats
The spaces between
The fore edges of the solid notes
The hind edges of the same
The soft edges about
O Sing

Articulate
Enunciate
Define by letter
Letter by letter
The whole
The series
Skip the meaning
Find the spirit
The soul
Essential essence
The meat thereof (especially the meat, brother)

Find
Explore
Expand
Embroider
Build upon
Contract
Rebuild
Letter by letter
The parts
Into a whole
(so long as its the meat, brother)

33

SING THAT MEAT
MEET THAT SONG
SING THE BEAT
BEAT THOSE NOTES
VOICE THE ESSENCE
BLOW THE THING
PUSH IT HIGH
WIDE
DEEP
AND HANDSOME
Oh My Brother
SING YE
SING

Sestina Modi

34

Belfast, ME,
1978

bashi-bazouks
pozzy-wallah
pootly-nautch
wally-gowdy
poppa-loppa
quia-quia

quia-quia
bashi-bazouks
poppa-loppa
pozzy-wallah
wally-gowdy
pootly-nautch

pootly-nautch
quia-quia
wally-gowdy
bashi-bazouks
pozzy-wallah
poppa-loppa

poppa-loppa
pootly-nautch
pozzy-wallah
quia-quia
bashi-bazouks
wally-gowdy

wally-gowdy
poppa-loppa
bashi-bazouks
pootly-nautch

quia-quia
pozzy-wallah

pozzy-wallah
wally-gowdy
quia-quia
poppa-loppa
pootly-nautch
bashi-bazouks

bashi-bazouks quia-quia
pozzy-wallah pootly-nautch
wally-gowdy poppa-loppa

There is no reason why the subject matter of art should be held fast to the plane of a working surface or be forever restricted by frames when there are so many possibilities for explosion, action and variety within the

composition and adjacent space. If these results can be obtained at
the expense of a few century-old fixations in art procedure then so
much the better.

Curiously the keys to a revolution in art already
exist in well known works. The points of departure merely need
developing. For example, John Constable's masterpiece, "The Vale of
Dedham" (1828) is a typical climb-over-the-frame-and-fool-around-
inside kind of picture. An urge is immediately invoked in the specta-
tor to do just this very thing and quite happily so. Once inside one
promptly pulls a sprig of hay to chew and saunters on down to the
river's bank at the left after a cursory stop by the fire in the fore-
ground. On up past the bridge houses, across the marshes by the
winding stream, one comes to the village, staying to eye a wench or
climb the belfry of the church for a panoramic view, before passing on
to the beaches and bay beyond. Vast reaches of open sky make this a
fine day, and one which is not complete without a stop-over for tea at
the heretofore unnoticed cottage on the right, just prior to returning
to the outside and the hard museum floor. This six hour excursion is
begun and completed in a mental flash. It was an exceedingly pleasant
and joyous time, but for the rather embarrassing limitation that it
ended.

Max Ernst demonstrates in "Two Children Are
Menaced by a Nightingale" (1924) that such journeys into pictures
can be equally as pleasant and possess the added feature of a curios-
ity-invoking adventure which is never quite concluded. To get into
this picture one does not climb over the frame but rather opens the
little gate at the left and walks in. The fact that it already swings
outwardly on its hinges and is held in this position to the frame does
not deter one from mentally performing this operation. Onceside,
one is oblivious to the commotion among the characters depicted in
the foreground and stuumbling over the corpse-like pile of draped
solids in his path walks parallel with the wall down through the
archway to the rear and on to whatever awaits exploration. Through-
out every step of this imaginary flight there is question and an
indescribable urge to solve it. Having surveyed the first enclosure, one
returns promptly via the archway and again follows the wall, though
more closely this time to gain what appears like a more direct en-
trance to the courtyards of the distant church and citadel. It is only a
foil, however. The maze is such that to gain admittance is to return

to the very foreground and try the knob on the door of the bathhouse cubicle at the right. Failing this, and one was somehow certain in advance that this door is not meant to open, one squeezes through the keyhole half-thinking perhaps that this is the solution and therefore worth the inconvenience. Alas it, too, is only a temporary relief and one has to end by doing what he thought to do before opening that gate at first entrance, namely grasp the knob half way up the right hand side of the frame and literally open the picture's plane—in reality a door, if one will examine the space at the top and the cracked effect near the upper frame. What is behind this mysterious door is the reward of the entire experience. It may be another picture, revealing in full detail the forbidden area of the first picture. Or it may not. Perhaps if Ernst had his way, this second view would be an extra-minute examination of the minds of the menaced children or of the man and child fleeing from the nightingale—those figures atop the bathhouse who first directed out attention to the knob—and whom we trust will escape just in time to slam the picture door in the evil nightingale's face.

For the sake of innovation—and progress—as well as to make point number one, I suggest that there be a series of opening painted doors becoming increasingly smaller and receding deep into the wall behind artworks. Whether these interlocking panels, as in this case, depict the flight of the man and child or elapse into other and more startling episodes involving numerous enclosures and barriers is immaterial. At the hands of a true artist such emotional and physical fireworks would be intriguing enough. I for one would like to get lost in the varying levels of a similar pictorial device and never get out.

Counter to inward recession just represented and so highly developed by the Italian masters are possibilities for utilizing the other directions and dimensions *upon* the picture plane itself. Rudolph Brauer, Hilla Rebey and other members of the Non-Objective School are often more successful in portraying motion with their carefully balanced color areas and space than Duchamps did by solidifying motion into self-fusing static frames. Spheres of color in a good Brauer oscillate between a point thousands of miles behind the canvas and a point just two inches beyond the observer's nose, while other areas revolve within another on the canvas plane like fantastic engines of wheels. Wolfgang Paalen employs literal cyclones and

37

hurricanes of color which gather momentum before one's eyes and whirling at accelerating velocities finally leave the canvas in a violent explosion. These are the beginnings of motion on a plane— Duchamps, Brauer, Paalen. In the interest of revitalizing art subjects may I suggest for number two, a concentrated continuation of these phenomena beginning where the pioneers left off—a revaluation of the anatomy of motion and its depiction, starting preferably in academic ateliers with *moving* models. In an age of travel-time consciousness a static nude is an antiquation.

38

Of action in receding space and that upon the picture plane, any which leaps forward to the spectator is equally absorbing. It puts in reverse those mile-long views to the horizon so characteristic of many artworks. Popularly known as exhibitionism in cinematic optics and an advertising plaything where pitched baseballs and on-rushing locomotives are brought into one's very lap, forward projection is an old principle, long neglected. In the central panel of "The Triptych of Moulins" at the Cathedral of Moulins, Jean Perreal depicts the coronation of the Virgin against bright colored concentric circles. The motion which these appear to set up literally hurls the seated figure forward as if from the barrel of a gun. Neither the gestures of adoration by the supporting figures nor the crown held by the angels from each side over head constrain this motion.

Flying pigeons in "Trinity" by Luis Tristan (1624) and "The Assumption of the Virgin" by El Greco (1613) leave the canvas in their flight, while the Virgin in Las Roelas's "Virgin with Saints of the Order" (1611) projects forward. Closer study of the cloud formations, light rays and geometrical forms used by older masters in achieving what appears to be unintended forward movement would then constitute a third suggestion for future development.

Both convex and concave surfaces, pressure-molded projecting parts held in place with plaster from the back and compositions where forms interplay within the two extremes of forward and backward advance are possible procedures for injecting new fire into advertising and display, commercial design, interior decoration and abstract art.

Other possibilities obtain (suggestion 4). Splashing

over the frame or overlapping it and giving the appearance of spreading out to adjacent walls is quite feasible and wholly justifiable when the objective is the union of the artist's creative consciousness and the spectator's environment. The gate structure already mentioned in Ernst's "Menaced Children" successfully bridges the frame from supporting wall to picture plane. Certain canvases by Jean Hélion and Fernand Léger exhibited without frames and having many neutral areas near the edges like those of the supporting walls allow for such fusion. Paintings mounted between the floor and the ceiling by cantilever supports or separated from walls by socket arms which allow the free inclination of the frameless canvas at any angle also achieve this result. Where frames are employed and hung from a wall in the conventional manner, eye paths from the outside into the picture are obtained by overlapping the frame in one or two places with the picture's composition. When skillfully executed, these links to the outside give the appearance of both cementing the picture to the wall and of making the picture fluid. When the framed part of the picture is the core of the design and the radiating tentacles fade out gradually into the surrounding wall, the total effect is that of neither a framed picture not a mural but of a pliant, fluid and intermediate form of great interest. A promising field of creation exists here.

Commercial makers have already offered pictures with convex surfaces and certain parts of the composition pressed outward in a third dimension with the aid of cement or plaster of paris molded into the resultant cavities in the back. Artisans of the mid-Victorian era offered portraits of our stiff-collared forebearers on oval surfaces recessed deeply in the conventional rectangle shape. It remains now to experiment with the other variants of a surface—the curve, angle and shutter corrugated, the plane recessed, regular and irregular, symmetrically countersunk and unsymmetrically gauged.

Where a Jean Varda embeds sections of scratched and cut mirror glass into a plane surface for normal light reflection and design, pieces of mirror set in some of these special surfaces can be made to serve both as elements of composition and reflectors of designs painted on the *back, inside* surface of frames. Thus one sees around, in and behind frames and seemingly the very supporting wall itself. The overall effect of a single composition which recedes, projects, moves in two dimensions and supplies reflected augmenting tones from behind its own frame is something out of this world. In its last analysis the once simple picture becomes a miniature theatre stage mounted box-like on the wall or sideboard with surfaces, mirrors and motion-forms interchangeable with the season's or one's mood of the hour.

Finally, significant approaches may be made to the concepts of reality through further exploitation and depiction of the multiple image in art. While this suggestion involves more abstract notions than can be discussed here, Dali's "Phantom Cart" (1933) affords an exemplary springboard to a vast and practically unexplored realm. As the cart approaches the city, both its physical outline and form coupled with its essence of function and perfection project to the oncoming form and spirit of the city. These parts in projection are bounded by neither time nor space: they vibrate continually like light waves toward one another. Just prior to meeting, the elements are essentially preforms. When they meet or join the result is neither cart nor city. Out of them new forms arise. These are never completed nor are they after-forms until we as onlookers choose to stabilize them at a given point. Then and there they assume a something which coincides with our mood and our view of what it should be. If this particular form for a given moment assumes a nothing, we ignore it; the next person will either see a growing or a decaying thing and depending upon its truthfulness the same will be real to him. But to no other. Thus it is possible to have a new approach to the foundation of things, the reason for their existence, the truth with which they carry out that existence and the force for good which by their being they instill in things about them. The wholeness and the apartness are double images in conflict but the reason for the apartness is that a new wholeness may yet rise again. Obviously the forced combination of similarly fused and widely divergent objects via painting methods opens an entirely new world populated with yet unconceived forms not yet described in any vocabulary or language. No greater revolution in art may exist than that of artists suddenly forsaking the infinite variants of reality and turning to the depiction of things we have neither seen nor heard of.

I am saying, then, that there is no reason why the subject matter of art and the methods of its presentation should remain forever unchanged. A little innovation now and then is the laxative progress needs.

Blank
Verse

41

San
Francisco,
CA,
November 19,
1979

```
        ^ ^ ^ ^ ^ ^ ^ ^
        ^ ^ ^ ^ ^ ^ ^ ^ ^ ^ ^ ^ ^
        ^ ^ ^ ^ ^ ^ ^  ?
    ^ ^ ^ ^ ^ ^ ^
    ^ ^ ^ ^ ^ ^ ^ ,          ,          .

            ^ ^ ^ ^ ^ ^ ^ ^ ^ ^ ^ ^ ^ ^ ^ ^ ^ ^ ^ ^ ^
    ^ ^ ^ ^ ^ ^ ^ ^ ^
            ^ ^ ^ ^ ^ ^ ^ ^ ^ ^ ^ ^ ^ ^ ^ ^ ^ ^ ^ ^ ^ ^ ^
    ^ ^ ^ ^ ^ ^ ^ ^ ^
            ^ ^ ^ ^ ^ ^ ^ ^ ^ ^ ^ ^ ^ ^ ^ ^ ^ ^ ^ ^ ^
    ^ ^ ^ ^ ^ ^ ^ ^
            ^ ^ ^ ^ ^ ^ ^   ^ ^ ^ ^ ^  ^ ^ ^  ^ ^ ^ ^
    ^ ^ ^ ^ .
                ^ ^ ^ ^ ^ ^ ^ ^ ^ ^ ^
                ^ ^ ^ ^ ^ ^ ^ ^ ^ ^
                ^ ^ ^ ^ ^ ^ ^ ^ ^
                ^ ^ ^ ^ ^ ^ ^ ^ !

        ^ ^ ^ ^ ^
        ^ ^ ^ ^ ^
        ^ ^ ^ ^ ^
        ^ ^ ^ ^ ^
        ^ ^ ^ ^ ^
        ^ ^ ^ ^ ^

                ^ ^ ^ ^ ^
                ^ ^ ^ ^ ^
                ^ ^ ^ ^ ^
                ^ ^ ^ ^ ^
                ^ ^ ^ ^ ^

                    ^ ^ ^
```

No future book/book of the future is possible until it is universally recognized and accepted

that the human eye is a clumsy awkward slow moving and wholly cumbersome unsatisfactory reading machine.

that it bumbles along on type lines in bothersome jumps.

that each jump is seven eighths of an inch long.

that if the last jump is shorter or longer than seven eighths the confusion, stalling, adjusting is highly increased.

that to find its way back to the beginning of the next line it must retrace the same path just traversed backwards, diagonally follow and cross the long empty space between lines with another backward motion or drop down to the next line and trace it back to the beginning.

43

that indenting every other line would greatly aid the whole process.

that a break, dot, dash or identifier at the end of each jump, regardless of where it occurs in a word or sentence, would further aid the process.

that putting the significant content of each sentence in bold type preferably in color greatly aids high speed vertical reading of a page.

that printing of the past has never considered the human eye as reader.

that all technologies must now be enlisted to help the lumbering gimbet through its daily chore.

Found Story

___ ____ no more primitive people than ___ natives ____ New Guinea; locked ____ from world by mountain, jungle ____ swamp. Many _____ not ____ caught _____ glimpse of ____ white man.

Some roam _____ forest armed ____ stone axes. ____ live in _____ world ____ superstition ___ fear. Wives ____ killed when husbands die. Brides ___ bought for human heads. Human flesh ___ eaten.

But most Papuans, although _____ ____ ____ uncivilized, are kind ____ good-natured. They _____ ___ ___ rather be friendly to _____ visitor than be ____ enemy.

1 Among the most primitive people in the world are _____ _____ _____

2 The reason these people have remained uncivilized _____ _____

3 Many natives   never _____

4 Many Papuans still use _____ as weapons.

5 Upon the death of a Papuan man, his wife is _____

6 The price for brides is _____

7 Despite their savage state, Papuans are _____ _____

*"I'm sorry I can read,"
said Oscar Wilde on first
seeing New York's night-
lighted neon signs.*

A. The eyes are for grasping, getting a hold on or fastening upon; certainly penetrating, even comprehending, know-ing, understand-ing; above all feel-ing, *not* seeing.

B. To feel visually *is* the thing.

C. The inner spirit of things seen comes to the surface for the benefit of the beholder.

D. Let him who sees beware.

E. It is not the form in space, but the space around the form that defines, distills, lets go of the meaning.

F. Black is both elegant and subtle.

G. Let form effuse, bubble up, overflow, effloresce, sparkle, sing, shine brightly, reproduce itself many fold.

H. To feel a thing is to know it. (See also B.)

I. Soul sees and knows more than either eyes or mind.

J. Self-interpretation is essential.

K. Content is more than significant; it is an integral part of the one seeing.

L. Good intent always radiates outward and for just reasons. (See also C.)

M. Potentialities for constructive use outweigh pernicious elements.

N. Pre-willed, purposeful statement is self-perpetuating.

(juggle the order and re-read)

Sonnet
For An
Elizabethan
Virgin

47

Belfast, ME,
1980

oA oA oA oA oA
oA oA oA oA oA
oA oA oA oA oA
oA oA oA oA oA

oA oA oA oA oA
oA oA oA oA oA
oA oA oA oA oA
oA oA oA oA oA

oA oA oA oA oA
oA oA oA oA oA
oA oA oA oA oA
oA oA oA oA oA

oA oA oA oA oA
oA oA oA oA oA

Beyond the ken, the far horizon, action seethes. Up, down and around.

Without the view, nearer but unseen, decay hastens, as inside the range, up to the close at hand, sultry air undulates wearily.

It is a typical scene.

Meanwhile, light rays, embracing the remote and close, reflect replicas of their shape and form toward the open eye. Converging, the beam pierces the cornea, penetrates the anterior aqueous chamber to that ever open window, the pupil. Compressing still closer, it passes through the focusing lens and the vitreous humor, coming to rest lightly but in sharp, inverted detail upon the most sensitive of recording screens, the retina. Sight impulses simultaneously surge along the optic nerve to the decoding room in the brain.

"It is a normal view," is the instant rejoinder.

"Untidy, therefore best forgotten," concludes reason.

Thus dismissed, the combined thought and sight currents trickle back to the retina as lights along the opto-sensory halls dim behind them and the mind, bored with browsing among incidental thoughts and scenes, slithers across the bony ceiling of the skull to sleep among the crags.

49

Still registering in full detail, but unseen, the focal center of the external view drops below the nose, leaving a space through which the eyes seek distant nothing. As the absolute greyness of infinite space vibrates before the now gaping doors of the forehead, falling discs of liquid transparency record each oscillation. When knowledge of their volatile but persistent presence permeates that drowsy vastness within, the mind rouses.

"Black out," it snaps, writhing.

Thought stages and whole stacks of unconnected ideas collapse from the reverberations of the sharp order. The already nonrecording sight nerves further ignore and blur the retina images as they busily erect opaque barriers against the falling spots and oncoming reflections. The unseeing eyes, immobile, fail now to register even the dead grey of nothingness as, unsuspended within the vacuous skull, the mind returns to sleep. Outside, the undulating air congeals into a single wave spanning infinity and the nose-bridge.

Nothing begets nothing.

One simply gazes.

Black. White.

50

Found Poem,
Belfast, ME,
1977

Black. White. Black. White. Black. White. Black.
White. Black. White. Black. White. Black. White. Black.
Black. White. Black. White. Black. White. Black. White.
White. Black. White. Black. White. Black. White. Black.
Black. White. Black. White. Black. White. Black. White.
White. Black. White. Black. White. Black. White. Black.
Black. White. Black. White. Black. White. Black. White.
White. Black. White. Black. White. Black. White. Black.
Black. White. Black. White. Black. White. Black. White.
White. Black. White. Black. White. Black. White. Black.
Black. White. Black. White. Black. White. Black. White.
White. Black. White. Black. White. Black. White. Black.
Black. White. Black. White. Black. White. Black. White.
White. White. White. White. White. White. White. White.
White. White. White. White. White. White. White. White.
White. White. White. White. White. White. White. White.
White. White. White. White. White. White. White. White.
White. White. White. White. White. White. White. White.
White. White. White. White. White. White. White. White.
White. White. White. White. White. White. White. White.
White. White. White. White. White. White. White. White.
White. White. White. White. White. White. White. White.
White. White. White. White. White. White. White. White.
White. White. White. White. White. White. White. White.
White. White. White. White. White. White. **White.**

Persons who feel, comprehend, know, understand through their eyes find great excite- ment in the found arts.

Persons who comprehend, know, understand through their minds find it a total dud of nothing and walk off without so much as giving half a try.

Persons whose five senses are not dulled, bruised, warped, wounded by the terrible forces inflicted upon them from the outside can feel and know through their eyes, fingers, nose, ears and taste.

Persons growing like the flowers of the field as nature intended find finding and seeing founds an exciting thing.

Under such restrictions it is obviously confined to smallish groups, say children up to twelve, adults of native and natural peoples, that is to say those unexposed to education, mass media, governments, and the world about.

Things of mine are meant to be touched, sensed but not read or understood mindwise, though pronouncing out loud is useful.

52

Asbestos

Baie Comeau
Calgary Alta
Dismal
Edmonton Dig
Flat Bay Junction
Gaff Topsail
Hawesburg Hull
Isle Au Haut
Jonquiere
Kelligrews
La Tugae
Moonbeam
New Sarepta
Ogahalla
Pontypool
Quebec Local
Rouyn-Noranda
St. Tite
Talbot Club
Utica
Vanleek Hill
Whitemouth
Xinon
Yarbo

Ziam

FOUND SOUND

Specifications:
1. Ask for anything to read
2. Ask for any number of things which make sounds
3. Start reading and sound production slowly, with feeling
4. Modulate and build up to a crashing roar

PREPARED FOUND SOUND

Specifications:
1. Ask for anything to read
2. Collect on tape short sequences of all manner of sounds
3. Start reading and mixing the collected sounds, slowly, with feeling.
4. Modulate and build up to a crashing roar

PREFERRED SOUND FOUND

Specifications:
1. Produce silence
2. Loll in it

FOUND POEM SOUND

Specifications:
1. As above using a found poem

PREPARED FOUND POEM SOUND

Specifications:
1. As above using a found poem

PREFERRED SOUND FOUND POEM

Specifications:
1. As above compounding the silence into prolonged blanks of non-vibration

ACTON VALE
BLUE MUCK
CORN BUD
DOD DOG
EAR HEAD
FLIN FLON
GLEN RIGG
HIGH LEVEL
IRON BRIDGE
JUMPING PEA
KELLY NOSE
LOW BUSH
MOON BEAM
NORTH PORCUPINE
OAK BAR
PICKLE CROW
QUEER SPRING
RED DEER
SAVANT LAWN
TATTA SONG
UKLE COVE
VAL DAVID
WHITE FOX
XION COLD
YARBO SIDING
ZAM DOCK

Many Have Heard Words

1. Many have heard words. Few have heard their meaning, sense and music. Many words are now so bruised in our culture that only their music remains. Let us listen to them. Do take time.

2. Sounds have been heard by all of us. But have you also heard their spirit, their inner being? Out of noise comes harmony; from discord issued the neat. The solitary bloomed. The conglomerate broke down. Respond.

3. Non-instruments crystallize their truth only when beaten, blown, scratched and belted. Instruments have greater ranges than designers intended. Employed in concert the non and the real make both real and non. Surrender.

4. Comraderie, three to six, together, spontaneous, unrehearsed, foot to jowl, manufactures the intuitive output, magical, beautifully rough, uneven but clean, always pure.

5. Into its own, never concealed, comes the fullness. Our senses dulled beyond repair in this hub-a-dub world, how pleasant to feel them rehealing!

6. Uncluttered, detached, separated from the others, then mixed into a whole only to be broken again, speeded up, slowed down, now high then low—never mind the mind—let the soul feel it.

The Card Index Song For The Filing Sisters

A Aa Ali Ame Ardo Az
Ba Bamo Biom Boyl Bra Btm Bs
Cep Chi clm Cmno Cpr Cqs Ct Cye Cx

D Dag Dimh
Ele Epe
Fri Fro Frm Frp
Gh Ghi Gr
H Heq Hrf Hst Huz Hy
Ip Iq
J
Kia Kpm
Lim Lin Liq
Megi Megg Midi Mie Mye Mysm
Nih Nylq
Op Ope Opa Oq
Pel Pda Pik Prl Prp Psn
Qt Qu Qy
Rik Riln
Sby Sca Shu Si Sja Sk
T Tn Tqa
Um Uop
V
W Whi Wj
X Xx
Ym Yn Yo Yp Yq
Zz

Finite worlds of infinite reality and beauty revealed by the tools and discoveries of Science are ripe for aesthetic development.

1. Of light, besides the commonly employed natural and artificial, there is the polarized, the radiating chemical, mineral and radioactive types along with x-ray, cosmic and nuclear-particle beams with all related electro-optical phenomena.

2. Of other vibrations, there are the natural, the mechanical oscillatory, resonant and supersonic sound, the entire frequency range of electrical and thermal waves.

3. Of movement, there is mechanical and electrical acceleration to light speeds; nuclear, gravitational and magnetic interactions, the mechanics of flow and change in matter.

4. Of phenomena, there is hysteresis, electrolysis, isotopy, relativity, entropy, et cetera; of devices there is no end: cyclotrons, stroboscopes, cynometers, spectroscopes, cloud chambers, tonometers, diffraction gratings, x-ray tubes, electron microscopes, et cetera; likewise phases of Science e.g. meteorology, hydrostatics, crystallography, histology, aero-dynamics, astrophysics, metallurgy, et cetera.

From such as these, their similar related effects, the manifold variants they suggest, stem the heretofore unrealized textures, patterns, forms, devices and techniques comprising SCIART.

The depiction of these individual materia by conventional methods forges new reality particularly when expressed on non-rectilinear shapes having other than plane surfaces and with media not normally employed in art.

Such combinations as photography and art (photograms), topography and portraiture (map blank-outs), photography and poetry (photo-poems), calculus and sculpture (math-forms), drawing and poetry (poemscopes, poster poems), biology and art (bone sculpture, painting), and aerial photography, geology, biology and painting (dyneton, amorphous, spiritism and non-rectilinear art) suggest the already fertile potential auguring continued exploitation.

P l o t

60

Found Poem,
Belfast, ME,
1992

```
> x
[1] "fred"    "harold"
#z as modified after call to "caps"
> z
[[1]]:
[1] "Fred"    "Harold"


[[2]]:
[1] 2



        > a
        [1] 5 6 2 8
        > b
        [1] 2 3 7 7
        > lg <- larger (a,b)
        > lg
        [1] 5 6 7 8



larger <- function (x,y) {
        y.is.bigger <- x < y
        x[y.is.bigger] <- y[y.is.bigger]
        x
}
```

61

```
if (...) {expr}  else (...) {expr}
switch
for (i in ...)   {expr}
while (cond) {expr}
repeat    {expr} <for infinite loops>
&    &&    |    ||
>  <  >=  <=  !=
```

```
> plot(co2, pch=2, axes=F,
```

```
> plot(my.co2)
```

Michael Angelo, artist supreme, instructed his students: "If you would create, relax before moldy, wet walls and feel form shaping out of the chaotic patterns."

"Designs in the grain of wood near my bed enfolded into figures that haunted my childhood," says Max Ernst, surrealist.

"My parents were startled by my ability to discern several more animals in picture puzzles than the artist intended. Oftentimes my discoveries were better defined than the one he hid intentionally in the maze of lines," boasts Salvador Dali.

Thus feeling would appear to precede seeing; feeling involves direct contact with an External.

It is this beginning or source spring that eludes, yet feeds, complete awareness.

The artist cannot say, "Now, I shall paint a picture," nor the scientist assert, "Knowing molecular behavior, I shall this moment compound the source of life." Both acts are purposely set beyond the pale of immediate behavior.

Theories of symmetry, color and movement; equations of radiation, electromagnetics and space, while they draw their manipulator closer to the borderline of the known and the unknowable, do not permit full compass of that barrier. Its pre-glow merely humbles the would-be onlooker, prompting him to so order his faculties that further exposure to the awesome stillness may be his reward.

Pictures and discoveries automatically take care of themselves from that point forward.

The secret of this approach to creation lies in Michael Angelo's admonishment: RELAX.

To "feel semblances in chaotic form" is merely relaxation as it applies to the artistic temperament and is best illustrated by Dali's daily ritual wherein, abed during the twilight zone of sleeping and waking, he dons a driver-like helmet and "doodles," pencil in hand, until significant forms emerge, requiring further development under a ready head-light. Ernst's methods are more simple to emulate as they derive from the silent contemplation of Nature as preserved in New York's Museum of Natural History. In both instances the artists first get in tune with a beginning as it arises from non-forms of nothing and the infinite variants of the commonplace— all elements close to the External.

The scientific approach probably does not differ radically. While it has always preferred to shroud itself behind closed laboratory doors and advance under the sheer momentum of equations, apparatus and reagents, its greatest contributions result when the precision of cold logic gives way to controlled feeling. This in turn is either External Motivation in action or pure inspiration fermenting by proximity to it.

64

Pure feeling born of a relaxed state is that "out of the blue" from which creation springs.

Myrtle Beach Before And After The Storm

wW wW wW wW wW

wW wW wW wW wW

wW wW wW wW wW

wW wW wW wW wW

mM mM mM mM mM

mM mM mM mM mM

mM mM mM mM mM

mM mM mM mM mM

Far, Far Away And Out In Front So Very Much So

for Walt Whitman

Old Walt
You're still in there
So firm, so steadfast
The ad-lib artists, the bibliographers, the copyists, the compilers, the critics, the churchmen, the detractors, the do-gooders, the hangers-on, the half-righters, the imitators, the politic generale, the pseudos, the reviewers, the reclassifiers,
the uplifters, those ever up and at-em boys

et al

(the whole shooting shebang)
Can not, indeed have not
       (though they certainly can't be defaulted
       for trying, lo these many years)
Dethroned, that is unseated you
Or even so much as unnerved you

You're out beyond now

Always were

Far from range

In outer word **space**

The Last Acts Of Saint Fuckyou

The abnegating of treaties
The acidifying of alkalis
The affiliating of bastards
The aligning of booby-traps
The ambulating of cripples
The annulling of covenants
The assessing of polls

The baiting of suckers
The beating of bare-asses
The banishing of believers
The bilking of swindlers
The breeding of monsters
The brining of sweets
The busting of influence

The camouflaging of enemies
The castrating of males
The causing of disasters
The certifying of devils
The clogging of conduits
The coloring of statistics
The cross-breeding of delinquents

The declaring of treason
The deducting of nonallowables
The deflowering of virgins
The defoliating of positions
The depreciating of standards
The dispensing of allergies
The distorting of basics

The edifying of traitors
The effacing of documents
The elapsing of contracts
The elevating of expectations
The enjoining of opposites
The extolling of crime
The exuding of stenches

68

The fermenting of riots
The firing of bins
The flouting of justice
The flunking of brilliants
The foreclosing of mortgages
The foreshortening of hymens
The framing of innocents

The gassing of stalwarts
The getting of bribes
The goading of downtroddens
The gowning of nudes
The grabbing of succulents
The grading of dropouts
The griming of runways

The hacking of corpses
The halving of totals
The harassing of taxpayers
The heeding of irrelevancies
The higgling of principles
The hosing of affluents
The humiliating of officials

The idling of servants
The igniting of fires
The immolating of nuns
The impeaching of innocents
The implying of gloom
The improvising of traps
The imputing of sins

The jabbering of smut
The jacobinizing of Baptists
The jamming of frequencies
The jaundicing of springs
The jibbing of progress
The jobbing of pot
The jockeying of funds

The kecking of wines
The keelhauling of delinquents
The kenning of gossip
The kicking of publicans
The killing of civilians
The kindling of rages
The kiting of bills

The lacerating of boils
The lacqueying of sleepwalkers
The lading of backs
The lamming of widows
The lapidating of humans
The laying of pits
The liberating of demons

The machinating of designs
The mazing of clarity
The menacing of enfants
The metastasizing of tumors
The milking of treasuries
The minimizing of importants
The multiplying of vermin

The naming of misers
The napping of covers
The narrating of contradictions
The naturalizing of criminals
The nidificating of vats
The non-prossing of plaintiffs
The non-plussing of laities

The obfuscating of patrons
The obligating of commoners
The obsessing of zealots
The obtunding of blades
The occurring of misfortunes
The originating of grievances
The overriding of objections

The padding of claims
The palliating of excesses
The pandering of lusts
The paralyzing of arteries
The poaching of game
The polluting of drains
The purveying of deceptions

The queering of sexes
The quelling of righteousness
The querying of innocents
The quibbling of facts
The quintupling of births
The quitting of scenes
The quoting of doom

The rabbling of mobs
The radiating of hate
The raffling of studs
The rankling of wounds
The raping of Europa
The recognizing of lesbians
The reselling of contraceptives

The salting of sores
The sacking of altars
The sanctifying of evils
The scaffolding of baptisteries
The shattering of nerves
The shifting of blame
The snatching of lightbulbs

The tabulating of thieveries
The teaching of adultery
The tempting of virgins
The terrifying of dreamers
The tightening of girdles
The tinging of heirlooms
The twisting of arms

The ulcerating of pimples
The ululating of laments
The unbarring of vaults
The unbuckling of stays
The underpaying of supplicants
The unfrocking of bishops
The unleashing of serpents

The vacating of leases
The validating of forgeries
The vanquishing of warriors
The varnishing of reality
The vaunting of lies
The vouching of makeshifts
The vulgarizing of priests

The wading of reservoirs
The waging of revolutions
The waiving of vetoes
The warding of peace lovers
The weighing of doubts
The wrecking of matches
The wringing of debts

The xerographing of copyrights
The xeroxing of xeroxes
The x-ing of entries
The x-radiating of negatives
The xylographing of obscenities

the xylophoning of dirges
The xystering of skulls

The yammering of joys
The yapping of gossip
The yarding of parishioners
The yielding of victories
The yoking of unequals
The yowling of greetings
The yuling of Easter

The zeroing of gains
The zesting of misery
The zinging of drums
The zipping of stays
The zooming of dirigibles
The zoning of beaches
The zounding of **oaths**

3

Whenever contemplating
the position of the serious
writer in this maelstrom of
coin and pulp, I grow
delirious and speak glibly
in extinct tongues.

In 1920 I started making books. Up in Maine my problem was the simple act of reproduction. In those days, Xerox had not arrived and mimeograph was very crude— certainly too expensive for me, and rubber stamps had not yet come in or certainly were not available in Maine, so my problem was to draw them by hand. This meant writing, printing the text and making the illustrations, and it meant an edition of five copies, an incredible work in terms of hours and of effort.

The trick was then to condense, to redigest, to state and to hand-letter and to hand-illustrate an edition of five copies. My first such book was done in 1920. It was hand-sewn, hand-drawn, hand-lettered, and it had a slip-case which was also hand-made. And since I had difficulty with titles in those days, I simply called them numbers, like 179B, and the next book, of course, was CD21. Thus, every title had at least one number and one initial.

My audience was a woman who lived down the street about four blocks, and when I completed a book, I would take it down to her, and she would give me a dozen eggs which I would take back to my mother. So I was making artists' books in those days—one book for a dozen eggs—a sort of barter system, the lady who received, my mother who received, and I who made it received no money.

I continued with this edition of five, and as far as the woman who swapped the eggs for the book, some friends from Boston would come to visit her in the summer and she persuaded them that they should give me the magnificent sum of one dollar and would take one of my books and take it back to Boston and take it into a gallery to some of their art friends and see if there were anyone in Boston who would like to swap hand-made books. My first out-of-Maine client, I've forgotten his name, was also making a kind of art book (I don't think they were as sophisticated as mine) but he was playing with words and putting them on numbers. Those were very rich years, 1920-1921, in Maine with swapping and bartering and the man in Boston who sent the books to some folks in Philadelphia, who bought some books, and the next thing you know they were tied up as far as New Mexico after about a year and a half of production. At no point were the editions more than five copies. I've been told that one of these editions that I produced in those days now sells at auction for $750, somewhat different from a dozen eggs which in those days sold for about 30 cents.

Publishing
Poems

When I embossed poems in virgin white on the colored squares of checker and chess boards the players said it confused their vision.

When I carved poems on the playing pieces they complained of a feeling clammy to the touch.

When I inscribed poems in color on the white square playing areas they grumbled of eyestrain.

When I engraved them intaglio they said the spurs caused sticking that required unnecessary lifting and placing.

When I printed the words guaranteeing no raised surfaces, no adhesions, they shouted enough.

When I approached the manufacturers of the board they said it was contrary to tradition.

When I visited the manufacturer's bankers they replied it's no margin of ours.

The distributors grunted no markets, the wholesalers barked no calls, the retailers said no buyers, the public yawned who cares.

The poets said no money.

But the commercials boys, the ab lib artists of radio and screen said ah yes, ah yes and yes but no poems. An ad jingle of course, but no culture please for literature is passé, dead.

Wailed the poets no money, no money at **all.**

Dear George Snell:

Since you have been so kind as to offer to give us our
first mention in the Chronicle after four long years of publishing, I
think it well to suggest one or two items which may otherwise escape
your notice. For example, our first publication was printed in
Knoxville, Tennessee, and published from Oak Ridge where I was
then a research physicist on the Manhattan Project for the develop-
ment of the atomic bomb. For purposes of secrecy of course, the title
page had to bear the word "Berkeley." Four days after its publication
it was seized and fourteen words had to be obscured by hand. It was
only a twenty-one page 3" x 4" item by Henry Miller, called *What Are
You Going To Do About Alf?*, and published in an edition of 730 copies,
any one of which is now very scarce and bringing, I understand, as
high as $7.00 per copy. While on furlough from the bomb project, a
second item came out from the address of my parents in Maine:
Angel Flores' *Chronology and Bibliography of Kafka*, an item which is
also scarce owing to the great interest in this important writer. A
numbered, autographed edition of Miller's *Plight of the Creative Artist
in the United States* followed from the Knoxville-Oak Ridge address
but with the Berkeley imprint. Being of Miller's first self-illustrated
volumes, it likewise commands fancy prices at this late stage. *Sem-
blance of a Devoted Past*, printed in New Jersey, brought many praises
by New York book designing clubs, and was judged one of the finest
things of its kind produced during the war, as was the Henry Miller
Miscellanea, printed for me by Greenwood Press in San Mateo and
formally acknowledged by the Rounce and Coffin Club of Los
Angeles in its current exhibits. *Murder the Murderer* brought FBI
investigations upon both Miller and myself and has since been
published in Australia, England, and France. *The Happy Rock*, a book
about Miller, which *Time* magazine said was composed by "thirty-five

internationally unknown intellectuals about a man no one ever reads, and all this on seven colors of paper," comes out in its second edition this month. The chronology and bibliography of Miller also appeared with his *Money and How It Gets That Way*, as did Parker Tyler's *Granite Butterfly*—a nine-canto poem adjudged to be the greatest long poem written by an American since T. S. Eliot's *Wasteland*. In more recent months, we have Philip Lamantia's *Erotic Poems* ($2.00), Leonard Wolf's *Hamadryad Hunted* ($2.50), and Kenneth Patchen's *Panels for the Walls of Heaven* ($4.50). Forthcoming publications include a poetry book by Kenneth Rexroth, an anthology of West Coast poets, an anthology of Spanish writers in exile, and art monographs on Zadkine, Helion, and Moholy-Nagy. In short, though we advertise in the Chronicle but have never been mentioned in its reviews, we are an established publisher featuring writers and artists who live and work within this immediate neighborhood. Our books are represented by Wayne L. McNaughton, Distributor, in this country, by Jonathan David in Canada, by Reed and Harris in Australia, and by A. M. Heath and Company in England and France. Our printers include the Packard, Greenwood, and Gillick presses all of this area, and Van Vechten and Waverly presses in the East. Most recently we have formed the Vanguard Club, a group of 500 people who by subscription in advance take four items as they come from the press. Membership is fast developing, incidentally, at $10.00 a head.

Under separate cover we are sending you the Lamantia. By telephoning Rexroth who wrote the introduction you can learn the full story of his life—of his protege under Breton, of his appearance in vanguard magazines throughout the world at a very early age, his editorship of *View* magazine, of Ark, and of the Libertarian Circle.

Since the Wolf and Patchen have been delayed by strike, I am sending versions of their books in manuscript and proof form, the thought being that you might like to prepare this write-up before Christmas thus being the first to review these books anywhere in the country. The books, we feel certain, will also be out before Christmas thereby allowing us to give you finished copies of the Wolf and Patchen on your return to us of the manuscript and proof. Wolf, as you know taught last year at the California Labor School, is a Teaching Assistant here at the University of California, and has appeared in *Circle*, *Accent*, *Occident*, and other literary magazines. He is only 24 and has an extensive war record. He has lived in Berkeley for three years.

79

You are very familiar with Patchen, doubtless, who at 34 is having his fourteenth book published next month.

If you are ever in Berkeley, I hope you will care to stop in or at least that our paths will cross sometime soon.

The Rounce and Coffin Club of Los Angeles—a high court of bibliophiles "having no concern with the commercial attitude of any agency, contributor or collector"—has just released its retrospective exhibition of the outstanding

books produced by Western printers during the war years 1942-1945. Many old-line presses have floundered and sunk in the morass of scarce workmen and materials, while other hearty souls have rid the dingy store-room racks of odd paper lots to carry on the western tradition of fine printing, producing small limited editions already out of print. Twenty-nine contributors from Idaho, New Mexico, Oregon and California submitted one hundred and thirteen volumes to a distinguished jury who selected fifty-five books of merit. Californiana and poetry led the field with a few texts and the two volume facsimile edition of the Charter of the United Nations concluding the array.

Most notable among all of the unusually fine productions shown, indeed, most significant of the entire country's book manufacture and creative output in many years was the work of The Untide Press. Of the war's twelve thousand conscientious objectors thirty or so banned together at Waldport, Oregon in a creative-arts program for cultural purposes. Among them were artists, writers, designers. It was but a step further to concentrate these diverse talents into the creation of beautiful pamphlets. A press was acquired from their collective meager sources and after the long grueling hours of "slave labor on projects of non-national importance" they gave their time and energy freely to this end. The artists' drawings were mass produced in non-union shops, the paper was the fine, odd-lot grades, the type and press second-hand and antiquated, the job long and laborious. Thus the profusely illustrated and multicolored *Generation of Journey* by Jacob Sloan, William Everson's *War Elegies*, and Kenneth Patchen's *An Astonished Eye Looks Out Of The Air* came into being for sale to other conscientious objectors. *At thirty-five cents each!* Books made by superior automatic equipment and selling at six to eight times this figure are shoddy and cheap. The equivalent has never been seen here at such a ridiculously low price. Nor what's more, probably will again.

Meanwhile, great publishing houses in the East are gravitating into mergers and combines with the express purpose of making money. To make money means millions and millions of readers, that many readers means the lowest common denominator of literary taste, the l.c.d.o.l.t. means trash; to make real money from millions reading trash is to mass produce, mass production means bad, unillustrated standardized design, cheap paper, crowded pages, just-hang-together-binding; these things in turn mean every

counter in the country is glutted with books and people, the distribu-
tors are well-fed and the publishers are vacationing at Palm Beach.
One book of eleven-year-old mentality, spicy fast talk, seduction, and a
murder or two for this kind of set-up and a writer can retire for life.
Obviously the breach between trash and literature is daily widening
with the movies, radio and newspapers perpetuating the gap. The
writers, publishers and sellers for that range of creation between this
mass extreme and the academic outpourings of the University presses
are either giving in to the temptation of easy money or just dying a
premature death from lack of food. Either way they are forgotten in
less than a year.

Whenever contemplating the position of the
serious creative writer in this maelstrom of coin and pulp, I grow
delirious and speak glibly in extinct tongues. Some of the notions
brewed during these spells include (1) self-barricading of writers and
artists into the war's military camps to produce their own works after
the fashion of the Untide Press for direct sale to the few who'll wait in
queues outside the barbed fence; (2) concoction of a chemical solution
which after dissolving the ink on the pages of second-hand and trashy
books, coats them with a sensitive film upon which fresh, worthwhile
words can be registered by light projection and for later dissolution and
"re-lighting" if desired; (3) production of books on microfilm for
insertion into hand-size projectors, cost of same to each buyer to be
graduated in terms of his income, those of the highest earnings paying
the most and those of the lowest receiving their book films free; (4)
secret seizure of all magazines in the country for one issue, filling ad-
less pages with first-line writing and illustration—but with the same
gaudy cover for the same thousands of newstands at the usual price, in
order to show the masses what they *could* have for the same money;
(5) . . . but as I say I'm delirious when I think of the creative artist.
Besides there are ten West Coast writers waiting outside with their
mss. Some of these fellows have been disinherited by their families for
wanting to write, others are supported by women, many have not eaten
regularly for months, some are the authors of as many as seven unpub-
lished novels. Their fine work is begging for an audience. But who
would buy an unknown? And where can I get the funds to publish?
How can I give their books away? I'm delirious, I say. Or is it the
world?

I know nothing whatever about bibliography. Any that I have ever seen appeared useful but dull. Their compilers I thought were gentle souls too stupid for any-thing else but page numbers, volumes,

and cross-reference notes.

No matter. I undertook a bibliography of Henry Miller because I love him.

84

The tax-payers of this country paid my way around while I called on his many friends. I kept them up nights. I dug into their packing cases. I fingered behind the books on their shelves. I copied notes, pages and dimensions. I visited twenty-nine states copying references, sticking my nose in other people's business and being generally grasping but congenial. Anything, everything Henry Miller. I wrote librarians, editors and book-stores: some helpful, some grouchy and water-logged. Post-cards, wax records and stolen stationery were sent to remote places. Strange people answered me, some in full, more often they replied only in clue. These drove me mad. Raving in fact. I called in specialists and academicians; I enlisted stenographers and lay-readers. Together we struggled on, mainly getting bogged in our own stew.

All the while I was besieging Henry Miller himself with questions and counter-questions. I spent hours with him at Big Sur, examining, cross-examining, pleading, brow-beating and belaboring his memory for every scrap, parcel and crumb. I wore him out. I read every letter, ms. and notebook in his place. I exhausted the specialists and broke down the post office. The result follows: 82.3% complete.

If it is, however, rich in non-academic sidelights, future biographers may thank me. If they do not, then I thank myself. A fair job, I say: thanks to all who aided me. THANK YOUSE.

Of the vast lacunae represented by foreign magazines, obscure and defunct periodicals and smallish newspapers, I have nothing. World Slaughter #II chased H.M. from Europe—he left behind trunks of manuscripts, clippings and reviews. Perhaps the kindly souls who thrive on bibliomania will excuse my rawness and ferret out these items, making needed corrections and countless additions. I shall pay them a small fee for their services. Perhaps owners of H.M.'s watercolors will also submit the size, title, date and inscriptions for a listing of his artworks. With everyone aiding a really significant bibliography will grow.

Miller is a very complex person. When I lived with him I cooked meals, cleaned the house, had the girls in in the evenings, got to know him intimately. He's an old man now. He's 83, blind, hip trouble, operation on

his legs, blood circulation's bad . . . the fate of man. He's read
everything under the sun, mainly things no one else read, he had a
nose for it. He is a combination stew of Christian Science, Emma
Goldman, a little common sense, a way with words, a natural gift of
gab. He's the only person I've ever met whose written words are the
exact duplicate of his spoken words. Here's this man who looks to me
more like a dentist than a writer, a common looking guy, very shy,
very bashful, but when he speaks it's like a torrent, like a waterfall,
and there's no stopping him, no shutting him off. Fantastic imagery,
word flow. And he writes the same way.

86

I'd just write: Henry, we're a little low here in research,
gonna break down the equipment so there'll be a lull for a few weeks,
I'll be down. So I went down. He was sitting there in need of
someone and I showed up at the right time. I learned many things
from him and one of them was to enjoy what we have. This cabin
that he had was given to him free. No electric lights, no need for
heat, he had some clothes which other people had given him, and
some people were sending in food. His idea was to be thankful for
what we've got.

I can remember him taking his wooden salad bowl and spoon
and cutting up some lettuce and making a very complicated and
fantastic ritual of cutting lettuce, putting some mayonnaise or vinegar
on it, grinding it in the bowl and sort of singing and happy, let's
praise God for lettuce! It was a celebration he carried on his whole
life, not only with lettuce, with bread . . . he wrote a whole essay on
the meaning of bread, especially rye bread, the ryeness of rye bread,
the breadness of bread . . . here was a guy who understood to hell
what bread was!

On the other hand, he used people. An interesting
example was he needed, he felt, a thermos bottle. He wrote friends
post cards: Dear Friend, it would help my life a great deal if I had a
thermos bottle, I could make coffee in the morning and put the extra
in the thermos so that by lunchtime I could have some hot coffee, but
I'm stuck up here on the hill and I'm the world's greatest writer and
so on and so forth, would you please send me a thermos bottle? Well,
the thing that got me was he sent out twenty post cards to twenty
guys, and two or three weeks later sure enough in came the thermos
bottles. Mind you he needed only one, but goddammit there were at
least seventeen thermos bottles, each one a different size, different

finish, different color, a whole goddamn collection!

And I'd say to Henry, look, all we need is one. Now

that God has blessed us with seventeen bottles, let's give sixteen away. Oh no, he said, this is a gift of God, I'm the world's greatest writer, I need bottles, we're gonna keep these. I'm deserving of all of these. He pulled this off all his life, using people, he even used me but I always knew he was doing it. I'd knock myself out financially to publish one of his things and he would take the same damn thing down the street to someone else, and his argument was that anything he wrote should be in at least six or seven spots. It always bothered me.

I don't know how many books he's written but he's turned out a staggering pile and a fantastic correspondence of letters that ran ten, twelve, fifteen pages. He would sit down at his typewriter, he would just go into a kind of trance, and the next thing you knew he was going like a shot. Not stopping, not struggling, not erasing, not back-tracking, never re-writing . . . it just seemed to flow out of him. I published seventeen books in all and kept them in print all these years.

I got to know many of his friends . . . Michael Frankel, Anaïs Nin, Durrell . . . they'd come to see him.

Now Anaïs supported Henry for about thirty years with money and sex. By that time Henry had gone through about three women legally, gone through his mother whom he hated, but when he had met Anaïs in Paris she in effect said you go ahead, Henry, and write, I will see that you get fed and housed and sexed and money and you just write. It was she who subsidized and paid the printer for the first edition of *Tropic of Cancer* and who wrote the introduction and who stayed by Henry through thick and thin for about thirty years, while she was getting money from various men who supported her. It was a kind of inter-cooperation of friends who were supporting friends. Henry's whole life from the time he quit his mother's and father's nest in Brooklyn was this business of living on others.

Gertrude Stein and Henry were two geniuses who couldn't be in the same room. When I came to Paris I tried to be the intermediary. I would say, Gertrude, look, Henry's a friend of mine, he's been over here all these years, you're both from the States, he's sort of broke, why don't you pass him a meal once in a while? And Gertrude would say: We're very particular who we pass meals to. She said, I have an instinctive feeling for when people are using me and when they really need a meal, and I cannot conceive of a situation where I would help Miller however desperate he might be.

88

Knowing Gertrude was easy because she was a sort of Greyhound Bus Terminal in Paris. If you went to Paris, you saw first the Eiffel Tower, then you saw Gertrude. Everybody knew where she lived, the goddamn place was like a bus terminal, all the French intellectuals were there and all the American intellectuals. Her influence was tremendous. The list includes Brother Hemingway, Picasso . . . of course Gertrude and Pablo finally ended up in bed together. She preferred to be with women, namely Alice, but now and then she slept with men. She was bi-sexual but she was very careful. The one man who made it with her was Picasso.

Okay, so Henry has this natural flow and this natural stew and in the course of sending out these post cards for thermos bottles, he would send out post cards for women to come and live with him. Henry would pound away at his typewriter all day and when the evening would come, Henry would put away his writing and take a nap and then he was interested in play. Some evenings there were two or three girls there and Henry would always insist that the girls all be at least partially nude, so he would have what amounted to private burlesque shows every night as a diversion from the strain of writing all day!

And of course it was understood that when they arrived they would bring some wine. I'd pass out about a quarter to ten, but they'd keep going until one o'clock with just about everything and anything you could imagine. These were mail-order orgies because these gals, having read one of Henry's books, would get the impression that he was some kind of sexual master. It turns out he wasn't quite as sexual as his books implied, but he was still quite a master.

Lawrence Clark Powell, he and I together, started the Miller Collection at UCLA and it's a fabulous thing. One part of it is "Letters To Henry." These are women and the general effect would be: Dear Henry, I've just read your book, my mother

didn't know I was reading it, I'm eighteen years old, my measure-
ments are so and so, can you meet me tonight at so and so, can I come
to your home, can you teach me sex? That would be the general
contact. And this would range from young 18-year-olds to widows,
women from all over the country would write him . . . a staggering
collection . . . and Henry would save them all and write back when he
needed one. One of these days someone who's interested in the erotic
mind will reproduce those letters. In full, I hope.

89

Declaring read-ers are snobs or writers are simi-larly afflicted ig-nores a grievous condition. The in-difference of the first and the in-competence of the latter are feeding the deadly inertia and apathy now

engulfing us.

On the audience side there is not genuine interest in good cultural things: an interest, that is, which is measurable by active, increasing attendance and participation, frequent purchase, gift and subsidy. Indeed, interest in anything outside or beyond the sex, food, shelter, smoking and drinking level is practically non-existent. Worse, people no longer see, hear, smell taste, feel.

Death of the sensibilities reaches to and includes the creators. The few who pierce the barrier do so without freshness, strength or significance. Nowhere is there a competent novel, a good play, an important poem. Too many practice exercises are getting into type, behind the lights and over the air. Knowledge of craft, responsibility to the problem at hand, even clear sensitive feeling are all too soon glossed over and ignored. Somehow the exacting task of rewrite, polish and refinement; the biting, stringent requirements of craft; the form, the parts in the whole, the sound, the meaning—all these get substituted by facility, obscurantism and experiment.

Little mags are not accepted. No one supports them; few are equipped to read them. A strange variety of prestige is invested upon the wrong writers among their contributors. The editors, who are generally frustrated writers (like publishers), lack discernment, have a personal debt to pay, or become so dulled by voluminous, continually arriving crud that they will take anything. Mediocrity and incompetence are perpetuated. And almost invariably from the same "names." Only a meager few among the great number said to have been born in the pages of the little mag are first of all persons, and secondly, sensitive recorders of five-sense reality. In short, all the literary atrocities heretofore associated with commercial publishing have seeped through the low-brow journals and on into the little mag.

With the public dead and the creators lazy, it is difficult to see how we can return to primal feeling, uninhibited awareness and an honest urge to express, to communicate lucidly. Perhaps physicists could aid the situation—and save face—by blowing up words.

Re: Pleasures Of
Obscure Outsider
Spending His Last
Dime To Publish
Living Literature

92

Huntsville, AL,
May 7, 1965

Dear Editors:

While browsing recently in a local bookshop I came
for the first time upon a paperback titled "Henry Miller Expatriate"
by Annette Kar Baxter and published in 1961 by the University of
Pittsburgh Press.

Miscellaneous pages skimmed over there in
the shop throughout the book's fourth chapter resounded vaguely but
not too positively until out of utter curiosity I purchased the volume
only to find on closer reading at home that the unfamiliar was actually
my own from twenty years earlier. In fact in 201 pages I found 63
short and long, accurate and incorrect references from a total of ten
titles which I had published circa 1944, each and every one taken
without my prior knowledge and/or consent. That I had actually
published 15, on, by and about Henry Miller at a time when he was
both destitute and unknown in the U.S.A. had gone unnoticed by the
author; with more patience she could have taken those too, sans
permission.

I noted from the volume she was apparently the wife of a
wealthy Sutton Place doctor and Associate in American Studies at
Barnard College, Columbia University, evidently a well healed
institution and like the press of the university in Pittsburgh well
supplied I would imagine with attorneys and funds to protect them-
selves even in cases of dishonor. Being small, outside and near broke
from my indulgence with living literature I have no attorney, or
funds, nor ever had; further I cannot legally contest this injustice
under these conditions. I can only publicly charge it off now as one of
the many pleasures of the small publisher presenting the contempo-
rary mode. Who else could be more taken by more illustrious takers
than Barnard, Columbia, Pittsburgh, Baxter?

Down With The
Manufacture,
Distribution,
Sale And Use Of
Guns; Down With
Hate

93
Rockland, ME,
June 5, 1968

A radio voice just said, "Let us pray for Robert Kennedy shot this morning in Los Angeles."

The voice did not say, "Let us pray for those who were not shot this morning." It did not say let us pray for the cessation of ammunition manufacture including purified uranium, isotopes, dynamite, gun powder, arrows and liquid flammables. It did not say let us pray for the total cessation of gun manufacture including Beebee, twenty-twos, forty-fives and on up to interterrestrial, orbital I bombs and germ vials. It did not say let us abolish hate.

Kenneth Patchen has been saying, writing, preaching and painting this message all his life.

Another radio voice said Johnson had taken authority into his own hands by issuing a decree protecting political aspirants by the Secret Service and waiting for permission to do afterwards.

94

The voice did not say LBJ had scribbled on the side of the wall, "I now herewith and herenow as Commander in Chief of all commanders do solemnly abolish in these great states the manufacture, distribution, sale and use of ammunition, classified and unclassified; do absolutely prohibit the manufacture, distribution, sale and use of guns; do herewith seize, confiscate and order all ammunition, all guns, dumped into the sea, the deepest sea."

Kenneth Patchen would have done this; has in fact been saying, writing, preaching and painting this message all his life.

Mail Art

ONE

The stamp fills the
paper
The ink fills the pen
All walls hold art.

TWO

Paper, ink, pen
Art needs the stamp
And another space.

THREE

Oh Art, Oh Paper
Where goes the pen
For another space?

FOUR

Wall, wall
Where is the paper
And the pen?
Bring us all together
This very day.

FIVE

Stamp, stamp
Paper and pen
Mail today.

SIX

Bring us the wall
A floor
Another space
We must say.

SONG

Mail Art, Mail Art,
Mail Art
There we are. We
are here.
      Mail Art
      Mail Art

4

The real problem was
Consideration, teeth filling
Love and fat purses
Were not of the same ilk
Were in fact you might say
Wholly incompatible

Rules:
A Found Poem

1. **Only** ladies are allowed to ask gentlemen for dances.

2. Ladies must not leave their dancing partners stranded on the dance floor, but must escort them to their seats.

3. Ladies may buy gentlemen drinks, but no propositions allowed.

4. Ladies must light gentlemen's cigarettes and cigars.

5. Ladies must use discretion and not try to dance with the same partners twice.

6. Ladies are cautioned against pinching gentlemen.

7. Ladies are requested not to use cheek-to-cheek tactics while dancing and should face their partners at all times.

8. Ladies are not permitted to tempt men with offers of vicuna coats and Cadillacs.

9. Single girls are at liberty to ask bachelors for their hand.

10. Ladies should select gentlemen other than their own **husbands.**

What Henry Miller Said And Why It Is Important

Over the years from among all the words, the situations, the events, many will redescribe, many will remember this sequence, that scene, another episode; others will write, pay tribute, deride, criticize, imitate, be influenced, read, reread as others applaud, rewrite, fundicate, expand, elaborate, editorialize, comment, cross-file, index, catalogue and annotate. From the root comprising his initial billion words an overwhelming several billion more will multiply at the hands of countless others until in the resulting morass of verbiage the essential even simple, unsuspecting but all significant core will still remain undisturbed, even lost:

1. *Sex is everywhere.*

   A. It is in the

air
bees
birds
city
country
earth
food
news
town
trees
streets
water
bed
songs
clothes
cars
factories;

99

clean

boys
husbands
males
man

B. And in   females   2. *Sex is*   innocent
girls   pleasurable
wives   pure
woman   natural
                         normal
                         wholesome.

enjoyable
fun
good
healthy

boring
damaging
dangerous   shameful
degrading   sinful
dirty   stupid
disgusting   taboo
dull   unclean

3. *And sex is not*   evil   *not*   undesirable
filthy   unethical
hazardous   unnatural
hostile   wanton
illegal   wicked
immoral   wrecking.
monotonous
revolting,

Contrary to the law, the church, the state, the tradition,

argue
discuss
dream

		give	
		have	
	can	indulge	
	does	partake	
one	must	perform	it.
	should	play	
	will	read	
		receive	
		share	
		sing	
		speak	
		think `	
		write	
		wish	
		desire	
		drive	
		power	

More important the urge to fornicate (by whatever means) cannot be appeased, chastised, cheated, corrected, daunted, dazzled, deafened, debased, debilitated, disburdened, decontrolled, decreased, decrepited, deflected, deformed, defrauded, degraded, denied, devoured, diffused, diminished, dimmed, disappeared, disappointed, disapproved, disarticulated, disassociated, disbanded, discarded, discerpted, disciplined, discontinued, discounted, discouraged, discreted, discredited, disengaged, disentitled, disgorged, disguised, dishabituated, disjected, disjoined, dislodged, dismembered, dismissed, disobeyed, disobiliged, disordered, dispersed,displayed, dispirited, dissolved, dropped, eluded, emasculated, erased, expurgated, extenuated, extinguished, extirpated, extracted, fecundated, feigned, fixed, fooled, frustrated, guided, hood-winked, ignored, improved, killed, overawed, placated, repressed, restricted, reversed, shattered, sublimated, substituted, transferred, tricked, thwarted, untangled.

And all this the lawyer,
the judge,
the sheriff,
the jailer,
the censor,
the custom,

the minister,
the teacher,
the politician,
the doctor,
the commissioner,
the young,
especially
the young,
must
know.

101

And know it not so much from the parent, from the cleric, from the teacher, from the medic as from an expert impartial OUTSIDER.

And in absolute confirmation.

Henry Miller treats sex for its own sake; neither apologizes nor glorifies its expression.

Orgasms

I want to have orgasms without foreplay three or four times every day.

MS/January 1980, p.67
Phyllis Chesler
"Motherhood Journal"

Day, the first

    py fffffffff
    py fff
    py fffffffffff
    py ffffff

Day, the second

    py fffff
    py fff
    py ffffffff
    py ffffff

Day, the third

    py ffff
    py ffffff
    py ffffffff
    py ffffff

Day, the et cetera

    et cetera py ffff
    et cetera py ffffff
    et cetera py fffff

PYFFFFFFFFFFFFFF

To Fall In Love

Feel her hair
Nibble her lobes
Pleat her brows
Caress her nose
Finger her nostrils
Fan her cheeks
Kiss her lips
Close her mouth
Rub her chin
Choke her throat
Shawl her shoulders
Touch her arm
Knead her elbow
Twist her fingers
Stroke her palm
Twick her nipples
Press her breasts
Plug her navel
Comb her pubics
Pinch her butt
Rub her crotch
Brush her thighs
Cap her knees
Kiss her vagina
Make her come
Bless her feet
Tell her **lies**

Sounds beginning with the letter "a" that arouse me:

AAIEERGH
aiaiaiaiaiii
AAAH
Aaaaaaaaaaahhhhhhhhhhhh
aaaaaaaaaarrrgghhh
AAAOWWWWW
Agagahh
araieeergh
AHHHHHHHHHHRRRRRRRRR
aaaaaaaaaiiiiiiii
AHHRRR

and "e"
Eeeeeunnnnh
Eennnnnh

and "h"
HAOW

and "m"
Mmmmmmmmmmmm

and "n"
noaccch
noooooooAAAHHH
naaaaowh
NNNNNNNNNGGGGHHHHHH
noooooooaaahh
nnnnnnnooooaaaaaaaaaaaah
NUGGH

and "o"

Ooooooooooooooooohhhhhhhhhhh

OOOOH

oooowwwwwww

OHAHHHHH

oaaaaaaah

OOOOOOOOOHHHHHHHH

owwwwwwwwwwww

OOOOOOOOHIEEEEEHGGH

ouuuuuuuuu

and "u"

uuuuuuuuuhhhhhhhhhhhh

uingh

uigggggh

and "w"

WHHHHHHHHHPPPPPPP

whaaaanggggh

WHAAAAA-UGGGGH

wha-ugh

WAAAAAAAAAA-OWWWWWWW**W**

Love
What Are
You?

106

En route,
1987

She is making love to you
He is making love to you
They are making love to you
      making love
      making love
      in/out/in
      love.

her parts are going in you
his parts are going in you
their parts are going in you
      making love
      making love
      in/out/in
      love

Your parts are taking hers in you
Your parts are taking his in you
Your parts are taking theirs in you
      making love
      making love
      in/out/in
      love

Your parts have hers in you
Your parts have his in you
Your parts have theirs in you
      making love
      making love
      in/out/in
      love

her parts are in you
his parts are in you
their parts are in you
    making love
    making love
    in/out/in
    love

107

she is in you
he is in you
they are in you
    making love
    making love
    in/out/in
    love

she moves hers in you
he moves his in you
they move theirs in you

take her	give hers	have her
take his	give his	have him
take theirs	give theirs	have theirs

    in/out/in
    Ok love, **love.**

Mr. A was much interested in the fetching Miss B.

Furthering his aims, he invited her to a Marine Drive night spot. She accepted and came along with a girl friend as chaperon, Miss C, and with a chaperon for the chaperon, Mr. D. . . .

As the evening progressed Miss B's cousin stopped by, her aunt from Yigo, and two younger sisters. Then there were Miss C's three brothers, four cousins, and one elderly uncle, who visited the table, ate food and drank drink.

To say nothing of those old friends of Mr. D's. . . .

And Mr. A? His morning-after calculations show:

Total bill—$64.75

Number entertained—27

Time alone with Miss B—3 minutes.

Dorothy And The Kisses Off Cuba

Killer the ship's hotel manager knew full well
Dorothy would come
Sit in the same chair
At the same table
Use the same crockery, the same silverware,
The same half-spoon of sugar
In the same tepid red tea.
Has she not been doing it for twenty-five years?
Would she not be doing it for the next twenty-five?
And why?
Because as Dorothy explained it all too well:
"You get kisses the like of which are not
Given in the normal walks of **life.**"

Economics

*W/CPL sks genrs BM 2 mk LV 2 wife
while husb wtchs must b cln disct
sncr 8" or btr. she blnd 5'6" Foto &
ph# a must POB 3061 Simi 93063*

If the color of your skin
son
is west of black
and east of white
it's not because
your voyeur pop
and your eyeless mere
did you wrong
but rather that
their ever loving
close considerate
and gentle mindful friend
Richard Milhouse Nixonhad just
run up the national debt another forty billion
sold all the wheat to Russia
raised the price of platinum Cadillacs to Arabia
so high they had to raise the price of oil to make
their quota
paid off some hush money to Liddy, Bebe and Bob
needed a few repairs on private shack out west
things like ceiling to floor wallpaper
goldfish in the well
sent another few extra billions to Vietnam
Egypt Israel et al
(but hoped to syphon off funds for the poor, disabled
and unemployed to drag in a few more yes votes but didn't
and they didn't)
needed a few more bomb carriers attack planes

and defense radars
plus found himself short of fuel oil for the White House
light bulbs tapes and candles for Camp David all
at a time
when that genrs BM all cln
dist
snr
with 8″ or btr
had the wherewithal
to pay your pa's and ma's rent
vitals
and soap
and
they did **not**

Etta Flora/
Margaret Eudine

If you had not
Had not
Not had
Died
There would
Could not
Been/have been not/none of
Those affairs
Near affairs
Misses
Near misses
Arrangements
Near arrangements
Things of the
Touch
The heart
Mixed with
Near words
Near acts
Real in truth
Visioned in mind
Dreamed by day
And by night
Hour, hours, hour
By hour
The touch of a back
To the back
The skin
Pliant
Soft
Suggestive
Wanting

What wanting
(My God, what wanting)
From the days of the first
That very first
The truly first
Mother's
In fact, before that
The dream thereof
Whilst lying there
Within the warmth
The mild moisture
Having it all
Supplied evidently
Without effort
Automatic
Instantaneous
Full time
Ever present
Without doing
Any thereof
Just fed
Womb fed that is
The womb
The womb
The womb
Who could leave it
Who can leave it
Depart that warmth
That shelter ultimate
Ultra and so
So
So

So warm
So complete
Satisfying
Replete, full
Full
Goodies incarnate
Full
(Out here, not, not full)
Not complete
Not sheltering
Not warm
Not
Not
So many nots
Too many to count
Name
Enumerate
Set down
Record
List
Make light of
Bitch about
Complain
(Accept, accept
You rat accept)
Acceptance
Is the word
Take it
Or leave it
This here is the world
Without breast milk
Breast softness
So pliant
Warm
Warm
And the womb gone
Gone
Mother gone

Wife gone
Near mothers gone
Near wives gone
Left

Groom's
Lament

She wanted consideration
He needed the cavities in his teeth filled
Surely such could be had
Was not consideration a Biblical concept?
Teeth filling an ancient art?

She sought love
He required a fat purse
Was not this possible?
Love abounds
Purses are a dime a dozen
(Though often flat in the middle)

The real problem was
Consideration, teeth filling
Love and fat purses
Were not of the same ilk
Were in fact you might say
Wholly incompatible

Hence they fought
One another
(May perhaps be still at it?)
And you know
What happens when fighting
Begins—there's just
No end to it
And in the excitement
Purses, love, teeth filling, consideration
Get lost, forgotten
So much so no
One knows what's

115

Happening, or why.
In short, the war
Is lost, not won
And the jig is truly up
As they say

So lament dear groom
Tear your heart out
By the roots if you want
There'll be no consideration for her
And some crumb dentist
Will give you a slippery crumb job
At a very high price.
And as for love and purses
Forget both of them
For the days of the End
Are close at hand
Just as the prophets **said.**

How It Is/Was

116

Belfast, ME.
1984

I don't kiss
Strangers
Anymore
Anyhow
She said, said she
Especially
That decrepit
Old worldly
Type
I went to
The altar
With awhile back
Only there
Was no
Altar
Just a
Broken down
Old beat up
Counter thing
With two femmes
In behind it
One the Justice
Of the Peace (what peace)
And a Witness (what for, pray
tell?)
Who made us
Both say
We'd bear it
To the end
Even if it
Broke us
Which of course

It sure did
And in ten
Weeks flat too
We were through
(Or at least I was)
And fully
Out of the
Marriage bed
Away out in fact
And on my back
All alone
In a bed
The long nights through
Every night
In the very
Next room
Just down
The hall
A piece
With one
Extra super deluxe
Door I
Allowed myself
To pay for
In between us
With her
Going in
One way
And coming
Out one way
And me
Doing neither

One
Except
That fateful
Day I went
In to pick
Our, her/mine
Engagement
Ring off
The dresser dish
And the wedding
Ring too, her/mine
The one
She said
Was too high
Not wide enough
Too too low
Wrong shape
Wrong color
Wrong price
Wrong size
Didn't fit
Her finger
No how
Anyway at all
And besides
Cost much less
Much less
Than what
she had lost
Totalwise that is
When they
Cut her
Social Security
For widow
To
Married

No sir
Yes sir
Five years gone
All gone
Gone
With no
Time nor
Reason to
Be kissing
Kissing
A snot tooth
Face like that one not seen too
much of **lately**

117

Making War
Not Love

1. **You** don't seem to care for me any more.
2. You didn't kiss me when you got home.
3. You got home late from the office again today.
4. You didn't say hello to my mother when you came in.
5. You're going fishing again and you haven't taken me anywhere in years.
6. You've spent all that money on golf clubs and I need a new dishwasher.
7. You read your paper all through dinner.
8. You've been cranky all evening.
9. You didn't say goodbye this morning.
10. You shout at the children all the time.
11. You didn't take the garbage out.
12. You weren't at the office when I called.
13. You never give me gifts anymore.
14. Today was our anniversary (my birthday, etc.).
15. You were flirting with that girl next door again.
16. I heard you promise Henry that you would lend him money again.
17. Your brother didn't even talk to me when he called, just asked for you.
18. Your mother called about why we haven't visited her, as though it were my fault.
19. You haven't smiled once all evening.
20. You look guilty about **something.**

Them
And You

THEM: (several ages)   Scream. SHOUT.
Scream. SHOUT.
SHOUT. SHOUT (even more
loudly)

YOU: Remove shoes slowly while looking in the direction
of the sounds.
Slowly consider throwing the shoes at the screamers
as they continue their screams.

THEM: More of same only still louder and shrill.

YOU: Throw shoes violently, one at a time, at the
screamers.

THEM: Total silence (ten measured minutes of it).

YOU: Start screaming, louder and louder.

Still louder

LOUD

A Lula Poem:
No More Anymore

120

New Sharon,
ME, 1982

I don't have anything to do with you anymore
      (that is anymore I don't)
If you come over be sure to call me up first
      (cause I don't have anything
      to do with you anymore)
When you are here I'm the host and you are
      only the guest
      (cause it's all no more anymore)
I surely don't have anything to do with you
      anymore
When the dentist of mine drilled, filled, cleaned
      my teeth, uppers and lowers, you
      didn't pay him
(I don't have anything to do with you anymore)
When my under-body-spray-for-rust man treated
      the bottom sides of my dear four
      door car you didn't pay him nothing
      at all
(I don't have anything to do with you anymore)
When the rent came due on my little big nest at
      the Birches you didn't pay it
(I don't have anything to do with you anymore)
When the yard goods shop had a sale you didn't
      buy any, none at all
(As I said, its no more anymore)
When I showed you the washer-dryer set I wanted
      you walked away
(sure is no more anymore)
When you didn't pay two hundred dollars more for
      our wedding ring
I didn't like it so very much
When you didn't, you didn't

121

And you didn't didn't, didn't you?
And most of the time didn't, didn't, didn't
So I don't have anything to do with you anymore
    With you   anymore
            anymore
            anymore

You, I
And The Elders:
A Lula Poem

122

Belfast, ME,
July 12, 1986

You and the Elders
Were here
All three of you
(With me, that made four—*my* chairs)
"How do you like the sculpture?" I asked
"I don't" answered one of the Elders
"Should we pray?" I questioned
We did
(An Elder prayed)
"I don't consider myself separated,"
      I explained, "because we were not together
        when we were under one roof."
"I favor reconciliation now," an Elder said.
"This meeting will mean nothing," he added.
"I favor her coming here weekends," I said.
"or going away weekends."
"You can't," the lead Elder shouted.
"I'll not be your part-time wife," you shouted
"My marriage is ended," you said.
"I'll not do anything about it." you said.
"I'll not go to court," you said.
"It's ten years now," you said.
"How long do you want the sorrow,
misery, strain to last," you asked.
"Everything I proposed was rejected," I said
"She says she is not running a board
and room place," I said.
"Do you want a Bible Study," you asked
"No," I said
"What does the Bible say about all this?"
I asked.
"It says what you want it to say," said

123

the Elder.
"Maybe we better pray," I said
An Elder prayed.
"And thank you, dear, for coming," I said,
Grasping and kissing you.
Then you and two Elders left.
I was alone.
Am still alone
Will be **alone**

The Kinds Of Love

124

Belfast, ME,
March 27,
1986

Oh romantic love
    have you gone, alas,
    from lover's lane, the
    movie balcony, the parked car,
    to the TV dinner and den?

Ah budding love
    have you thought
    it all the way through
    to the court scene
    and the barking judge?
    All the way?

Oh puppy love
    how grateful we
    all are it soon
    passes like a lost dream.
    Amen.

Ah and oh The Crush.
    The Crush, it presses in
    so hard it almost
    takes our breath away.
    Praise be.

Jaded love
    love, love worn out
    frayed on the edges
    and run down at the mouth.
    Oh.

Unrequited love
     not returned, given back
     stolen away like
     the ashes of woe.
     Oh, demon, you.

Narcissistic love
     destroy, throw about
     push down and not let up.
     What revenge, what
     not taking back.
     Oh. Oh.

Ah doting love
     love hoping to bloom
     linger like frost on the pane.
     Let it sustain, nourish and grow.
     Oh **helper.**

5

War is a mental disorder of the highest order, a public manifestation that all who arrange, direct, participate are madly deranged. The insanity touches us all and we have nowhere to go.

Leaving the dining room of the Faculty Club, University of California, after a more than pleasant lunch, I entered the Club's lounge, picked up that morning's edition of the *New York Times* to read not only that a bomb had been dropped on Hiroshima but also exactly what I had been doing with my life and talents the past four years at Princeton, Oak Ridge, Berkeley.

128

One physicist reader started crying, screaming in wild destructive frenzy and had to be carried out strapped tightly to a stretcher. Another, dazed, voluntarily stumbled to an asylum for relief. A third took off for Minnesota to become a dairy farmer.

Myself, I am still numb after thirty-seven years, yet strong enough to have lived since in Hiroshima, Nagasaki, Norway, Russia in a futile attempt to understand what took place that August day of '45.

I am very sorry Madame Curie and Lise Meitner did not keep their findings to themselves, that their facts ever got into the textbooks, that war makers pulled their ideas out and ran wild with them to destruction in the interests of nationalism and money.

I am even more sad about my part in it all, even ashamed, and do here now apologize to all and sundry, as if such as that could conceivably aid, even assuage my conscience now that time is too late; and of course my confessing does not help in any way, it is too late— the monster is permanently out.

War is a mental disorder of the highest order, a public manifestation that all who arrange, direct, participate are madly deranged. The insanity touches us all and we have nowhere to go.

Probe
For Higher
Intelligence

As you may already know, Doctor Timothy Leary is guest editing an issue of *Spit in the Ocean* from in jail. He is using our office as a clearing house for information on his theme: Communication With Higher Intelligence.

In order to get your views on the subject he would like you to answer the following questionnaire. Please send your replies to this office. I will forward them to Tim.

Ken Babbs, Production Editor, *Spit In The Ocean*

1. *Do you believe the concept of Higher Intelligence is a useful concept?* The H.I. concept, long neglected and only partially developed, is extremely important, urgently needed.

2. *How would you define Higher Intelligence?* H.I. is an all-inclusive, ever present and universal radiating, receiving, assimilating and using energy plasma.

3. *How would you define intelligence?* Intelligence is the quality of sending, receiving and manipulating energy quotients of data.

4. *It has been said the human brain is an instrument which humanity does not understand how to use. Comment please.* Humanity has been for centuries neglecting, ignoring and wholly failing to understand both the brain and its uses.

5. *Do you believe that the wide variations in human intelligence are due to differences in neural wiring (i.e., genetic) or due to social-educational differences? Or both?* The wide variations in human intelligence are due to all these factors: a) genetics, b) social-education differences, c) political forces, d) environment, e) food.

6. *Do you think that neural differences among individuals or racial groups define different sub-species?* Neural differences do define different sub-species.

7. *Do you think that the very concept of intelligence or differences in intelligence is elitist or anti-democratic?* Anti-democratic. Monarchs, rulers both ancient and modern have reduced all their subjects to either a common extremely low level of intelligence, or none at all. Richard Nixon has been quoted as saying his administration considered the U.S. public as eighth graders and has treated and ruled them as such.

8. *The average I.Q. (however measured) is assigned the index of 100. This means half of the population is below I.Q. 100, i.e. just barely literate. What are the implications of these statistics?* The implication of the present I.Q. method is that the majority is stupid, ignorant, incapable of thinking and much in need of being ruled, regulated, maneuvered, taken care of and provided for.

9. *Do you think that a level of intelligence exists that is as superior to the human as the human is to the ape's?* There very certainly are many levels of intelligence superior to present man.

10. *If so, in what form does it exist?* These higher levels of intelligence have long since broken the shackles of the prevailing five senses system and taken off into the sixth, to the twentieth, to infinite sense states.

11. *Do you think Higher Intelligence exists on other star systems in the galaxy?* H.I. certainly does exist on other star systems.

12. *What are the chances of our contacting Higher Intelligence in your lifetime?* H.I. was contacted in prehistoric and early Biblical times, continues to be developed, and will undergo accelerated growth in development and understanding.

13. *Do you consider DNA as an intelligent entity? Why?* DNA is an intelligent entity because it reduces to basic energy characteristics common to all intelligences.

14. *Do you consider the nucleus of the atom as an intelligent entity? Why?* The atomic nucleus is an intelligent entity because it also reduces to the same pulsations of vibrating energy plasma.

15. *Do you believe that humanity will evolve to a higher level of intelligence?* Humanity is slowly evolving into a higher intelligence but under tremendous resistance and negative forces.

16. *If so, what form will this take?* The present brain system will simply encompass the full potential for which it was originally intended.

17. *Do you think that intelligence can be raised?* Intelligence can not only be raised but must be developed immediately.

18. *Do you believe that the raising of intelligence levels should be defined as a national priority project comparable to raising the level of energy resources?* The raising of intelligence levels has a higher priority than raising energy resources.

Final H.I. Statement by Bern Porter

The pulsating, expanding, contracting vibrant energy plasma which I call intelligence, sends, receives, assimilates, manages and controls energy data bits within the confines of a present five-sense system.

Breakthroughs beyond these five were obviously intended in the original neural concept but to this date have been hamstrung and left bruised, even damaged, by prevailing political, economic, social, educational and environmental factors.

Men have the potential to progress outside and beyond themselves into even higher energy plasma or H.I.

All of us have heard of signals, code patterns being sent from earth, and earth listeners awaiting space people to receive, understand and reply. What we overlook while this notable, and perhaps some day fruitful, effort continues is that physics laboratories in course of intercepting, redirecting, smashing, exploding and lastly super-magnifying solid substances, find incredible spaces between atoms, and right here on our own earth level. What appears solid to the human eye, under great magnification is in reality a wide-open terrain of mountains and valleys, with fantastic spaces between peaks. The haunting question is what lies between? Non-human intelligent beings?

133

True, anything living produces its own radiation field or halo. With it trees, flowers, speak to one another as do birds, insects, animals, fish.

Besides wanting to hear what such living things are saying to one another, what great excitement to listen in on the conversations going on between the spaces of atoms!

Someday we know, though Einstein has assured us in advance, that the ultra-thin, expanding and contracting membrane separating us from truth, with its swinging-door openings, will allow us only momentarily to see through, or more likely never see nor know. What if stones, tables are talking to one another while the inner spaces of their molecular structures are alive with other sounds? It is a fascinating subject equal to any possibilities coming to us from planets.

Whenever I think of Einstein, I think of him as a little kid.

He would run around with dirty jeans and a turtleneck sweater and his favorite pasttime would be to play with the dogs in the street and with little children and eat ice cream cones, and he'd stand around on street corners and the people in Princeton just took the view well he's thinking, let's overlook that he hasn't combed his hair, he hasn't shaved, and his sweater is dirty with soup stains and vanilla ice cream . . . let's overlook all this stuff, this is a brain, this man is an incubator, he's thinking! He's getting close to the membrane.

An interesting example of this attitude is that a total of seven people waited on him. He didn't sit around worrying about the light bill and the gas bill and the grocery store and taxes and all the physical things that you and I go through every day. There were seven people doing all that, standing around just seeing to it that he was free to think. He was treated as a superbrain in an incubator. The Philharmonic of New York came down to Princeton to rehearse. Students and faculty members could go free, otherwise it was two bucks. Einstein was a musician, a very accomplished one, so he would go to these performances. But he would carry with him his cane and his coat.

He would sit in one seat, put his coat on his right and his cane on his left, and he would sit there occupying three seats with standing room only. Nobody would speak to him or interrupt him because he might be thinking of something, he was there to think. And who would dispute that while sitting there occupying three seats or running around the streets of Princeton looking like a bum, he might not think of something? In fact the general rules were that no one was allowed to address him, and to be sure a block away would be one of the seven to see that no one bothered him! He was treated like a little baby in a crib on the principle that here's a brain that must be allowed to think.

135

I was greatly moved by the passing of Dr. J. Robert Oppenheimer, as I knew him very well, and miss him.

He was killed by tobacco, and the world's rejection of his ideas. The tobacco which he smoked constantly seemed to help ferment his ideas.

I think he regretted having taken part in the development of the A-Bomb for explosive purposes only. And he opposed the development of the H-Bomb. He was against the use and spread of atomic energy for military purposes, and he wanted us, since we have the thing, to use the energy industrially, and for peaceful purposes only and for fuel, power, light, heat, etc. Like Dr. Einstein, he regretted that all this activity took him away from pure physics and into politics, government, etc., and far, far from the laboratory, where he was more at home.

He was unable to cope with the world in terms of "mass views" and even conducted his own trial badly, not knowing the *"mass laws,"* procedures, opinions, etc., and I think he never understood "the public," really.

Once caught in trying to save the world from what he had developed, he became like the windmill-fighting Don Quixote, with derision high on all sides, a pathetic figure in a way, yet noble if rightly understood on another plane—and the very picture of our modern tragedy.

At his death, he was writing a history of modern physics, and, I would judge, brilliantly, as his style was accomplished, articulate, and concise—rare in his profession.

But, most interesting, he became a symbol of:
a. One starting something greater than himself.
b. The scientist who changed the world—more than any can yet say or the ultimate consequences of which can't be predicted.
c. "The bewildered one" in a valley of alien forces.
d. The "father" physicist to a great many, including myself, on a very human level—the natural kind, which did not frighten common people, as was the case with Einstein. He stood high on an academic pedestal, yet was personally child-like.

Dr. Oppenheimer was a great figure to say the least, because he was scholarly, theoretical, remote, and far-out; all the while frail, stuck with common, oh, so common fellows, always outsmarting him in practical realms, while he led group discussions and experimental work through deep corridors of physical and mathematical thought. (Personally, he led me to understand physicists of world-wide fame and their work in our field.)

Sadly, his papers on pure physics seem to have been lost, figuratively, so much more sensational were the other aspects of his work.

Dr. Teller, by contrast, is an untutored farmhand,

uncouth, and far more confused by public forces and events that he, too, could not control, although he helped also to unleash them upon the world.

I think he was manipulated and used by militarists, governments, industrialists, and war cliques, who capitalized on his personal desire to have revenge against all seemingly Hitler-like forces, that had persecuted and killed his relatives in Central Europe. Dr. Teller, the insensitive, non-scholar, commercial type has collaborated fully, even if at times unknowingly, in the game of mass death, mass fear, and mass power, and when J.R.O. refused to play the same game, Dr. Teller calls him *"wrong-headed"* and *"idiotic"* as quoted in the *N.Y. Times* recently.

In contrast, consider Oppenheimer as the master scholar, publicly admitting his own flaws, but holding steadfastly to his principle of "a better world," and "a better society" through physics (technology), becoming more general as a result of scientific discovery (and throughout his remaining life.) The intellectual not to be eliminated, though having been the target of all the "anti-Powers," but reinstated as of equal significance with the other forces of industry here now.

While sheltered for 18 years in the warm confines of the Institute for Advanced Thinking at Princeton, J.R.O. was often invited to world capitals to lecture, or, more correctly, to expose himself to the verbal spears of the "War crowd" who sought to kill him and all he represented by whatever means, aided and abetted by a sensational "Press" too often on Teller's not J.R.O.'s side.

Few Americans were held in as much respect by European *intellectuals* as Oppenheimer; and plays, novels, and critiques abound abroad on the life, times and ideas of the gnome-like figure, which became his image. It required another *intellectual*, President J. F. Kennedy, to assure him even the smallest measure of U.S. respect by way of the presentation of the Fermi Award, presented belatedly and a little grudgingly later by, strangely, L. B. Johnson. A War-type and far from an *intellectual* man!

In prepared public expressions and writings, J.R.O. was without a peer, and made the commonly acknowledged oratorical master in their field, Winston Churchill, even appear second-rate, but how many readers of the modern press have had a chance to study his prose, or know what his general philosophical viewpoint was? Very few, I dare say.

Days In
The Early Eighties

It is coming out of the sky at me now
The fillings in my back teeth are loosening
The nails in the heels of my shoes are showing fatigue
My beautiful hair no longer combs like it used to
People stab me making deep word wounds
They leave scratches on my eyeballs
Their rancid blood in my soup
Radioactive ashes in my bed
Thrust rumors, speculation and gossip
Backed by press releases, news stories
Radioed and TVed into my ears
Leaving fear, doubt, questioning, uncertainty behind
All truths distorted, ground down, gone

I want to run but have nowhere to **go.**

Subject: Invasion
Of Privacy

141

Belfast, ME,
September 20,
1973

Postmaster Belfast, ME

Dear Sir:

It is the purpose of this letter to advise you as follows:

1. Information about my box number, street address, telephone and whereabouts cannot be sold by you for one dollar, for one dime or any other monetary consideration.

2. Information about my mailbox, street address, telephone, forwarding address, whereabouts or any other information about my mail cannot be given out by you without first having from me written permission to do so.

3. Information about my box number, street address, forwarding addresses and any other information about my mail and or whereabouts cannot be given to any persons whatever, so ever, under any condition, unless you first have my written permission to do so.

4. Information as above as to box number, addresses, telephone, whereabouts cannot be given by you to any police officers, state or local, to any agents of Social Security, Internal Revenue, Federal Bureau of Investigation, Central Intelligence Agency or any other agency of any type whatever unless you are first in permission from me in writing and unless and including said persons present to you in written form a court order to so divulge this information.

5. All of the above applies to verbal revelations, verbal remarks, phone conversations and written notes by you and all other persons in your employ.

It is also the purpose of this letter to advise you in writing, with all attendant responsibilities upon you, that my first class mail is being opened before I receive it.

142

> Bernard H. Porter
> Margaret E. Porter
> Bern Porter, Inc.
> Bern Porter
> Bern Porter Books
> Institute of Advanced Thinking

cc: Postal Inspection, Washington
Postal Inspection, New York
Postal Inspection, Boston
Postal Inspection, Portland
Postal Inspection, Waterville
Postal Inspection, Bangor

Most Of My Days Were Spent In Fixing People Who Had Already Spent Considerable Time Fixing Me

A&A	**He** aroused me: I abducted him
	He abhorred me: I abandoned him
B&B	He buffeted me: I broke him
	He bucked me: I buried him
C&C	He cajoled me: I condemned him
	He chastised me: I cheated him
D&D	He depreciated me: I debauched him
	He deceived me: I destroyed him
E&E	He extricated me: I extradited him
	He exhorted me: I expelled him
F&F	He frustrated me: I flayed him
	He feted me: I fought him
G&G	He graded me: I granulated him
	He greeted me: I gored him
H&H	He heckled me: I hurt him
	He humiliated me: I hackled him
I&I	He ignored me: I identified him
	He idolized me: I impeached him
J&J	He jangled me: I jailed him
	He jeered me: I juggled him
K&K	He kidnapped me: I knifed him
	He knocked me: I knighted him
L&L	He lashed me: I larruped him
	He liberated me: I lacerated him
M&M	He maddened me: I macadamized him
	He maligned me: I mangled him
N&N	He nauseated me: I nominated him
	He nudged me: I nullified him
O&O	He ogled me: I ossified him

	He oppressed me: I ostracized him
P&P	He pacified me: I penalized him
	He pampered me: I parboiled him
Q&Q	He quoted me: I quelled him
	He qualified me: I quailed him
R&R	He rankled me: I radicated him
	He rehabilitated me: I resigned him
S&S	He scolded me: I slew him
	He soothed me: I starved him
T&T	He tired me: I trampled him
	He tolerated me: I tyrannized him
U&U	He urged me: I undermined him
	He underwrote me: I unnerved him
V&V	He venerated me: I vilified him
	He vexed me: I violated him
W&W	He worried me: I whipped him
	He wrenched me: I wounded him
X&X	He xed me: I x-rayed him
	He xipped me: I xystered him
Y&Y	He yanked me: I yowled him
	He yoked me: I yapped him
Z&Z	He zed me: I zanied him
	He zested me: I zeroed **him.**

144

Run

In the interval
the side-line space
allowing forward
only

    RUN

the seconds pass
mounting time
in a ball
whose sum
denotes its passage

    RUN

the past recedes
grows dim
the sands compact
expand in a road
growing long

    RUN

the press is on
from here to there

    RUN RUN **RUN**

**With this ques-
tion as a spring-
board I shall ex-
pose what is un-
questionably the
greatest single de-
structive force in
our enlightened
culture. Moreover
I will call attention
to one of the most
aesthetically hid-
eous,** technically unreasonable,

the most scientifically inefficient, the most thoroughly ineffectual single device of our mechanistic civilization. I repeat, I will be referring to the American passenger car.

In the fraction of a minute I have been writing this section four people have lost their lives, seven people have been maimed for life, twenty-two people have been injured seriously, sixty-one people have gotten off with minor bruises, aches and pains. Four people, plus seven people, plus twenty-two people, plus sixty-one people equals ninety-four people dead or hurt, one of them perhaps your friend or relative or perhaps mine. Now the device that accomplished all this in a fraction of a minute weighed between one and a half and four tons, was traveling between 55 and 105 miles per hour, was powered by the equivalent of 190 to 290 panting horses and occupied as much as 1200 cubic or 220 square feet.

Is there anyone who can tell me why any automotive carrier other than trucks should weigh between one-and-a-half and four tons? Is there any justification whatsoever for any automotive carrier but a fire truck and an ambulance to travel more than thirty-five miles per hour? Is there anyone who personally knows of a road, incline or any carrier situation except that prevailing for trucks which requires engines equal to 190 to 290 pushing, pulling, panting horses? Is there anyone hereabouts who can justify the use of 1200 cubic feet when the person driving occupies between them no more than eleven cubic feet?

And while I am in this questioning mood may I inquire why with congestion, street traffic and parking an admittedly major problem are passenger automobiles made longer and wider each year? Some models go to 20 feet long and 10 feet wide. A sitting person covers a space two feet long and a foot-and-a-half wide. Is it not obvious that as thousands of more cars are produced every minute the bulk of congestion, traffic and parking problems could be eased by cars of smaller not larger dimensions? ...that less death and less injury from automobiles can come from lighter weights, slower speeds, less power? . . . that engine governors would automatically prohibit any car but fire trucks and ambulances from going over 35 miles per hour? . . . that it is superfluous to build cars for cruising when there is no place to cruise? . . .even sillier to build them to go 110 miles per hour when there are no stretches left in which to attain these speeds for

more than a minute at a time . . . that engine powers over 80 horses
are unnecessary for all but trucks . . . that weights over 750 pounds are
also unnecessary . . . that engines should consume one gallon per
every fifty miles instead of the present 9 to 18 miles per gallon . . .
that fenders, sides could be made practically bend and dent proof save
under the severest conditions . . . that cars could be made collision
proof from any angle . . . that cars made now for actual attention free
life of 4 to 9 months could be made to last a lifetime . . . that there is
no reason why the inside of a car should be an exact replica of the
living room . . . that a car brings out all the selfish, possessive, proud,
fearful and antisocial aspects of their owners . . . that with no place to
go at 110 miles per hour and no place to park the car upon arrival
makes the automobile really just another bauble fast approaching a
point of even less usefulness, excepting its major role in nose and
throat ailments via air pollution, its use or effect upon cleaning
conditions and dirt free living to say nothing of its use as an end to
voluntary suicide.

In this work I have endeavored to portray certain aspects of
a foreseeable future development arising from my thinking as a
consulting physicist. At this point I might mention a few more such
random innovations of my own devising. I have already mentioned
the obvious use of engine governors on automobiles that make speeds
over 35 miles per hour impossible. Further in this connection I direct
attention to the bat, a fabulous winged creature who can fly at great
speeds between the spokes of a rotating wheel without harming
himself, even fly between the spokes of two wheels each rotating in
opposite directions. How? The bat is equipped with a miniature
wave sending and receiving or radar set that warns it of the proximity
of objects stationary or moving and literally directs it away from
them. Such equipment on a car could be made to pass control
directly from the driver to the mechanism which shuts off the motor,
applies graduated braking automatically and affects a steering which
prohibits contact with anything passing within a distance of three feet.
If for some reason contact should occur under the momentum of the
original 35 miles per hour speed I am advocating then sides, ends and
fenders can be made bend, dent and crumble proof and even scar
proof without contributing greatly to the total weight. In short, if we
are intent upon engaging in the death game on a grand scale and
spending such sums for repairs as the $300 million spent in California
last year, there are means available for affecting some reduction.

But frankly these are only bad makeshifts for an already functionally bad device. If a passenger car is a means of getting the body from one place to another, and please take note that it is more often a primary device for exhibiting one's private means, a device for extending one's urges for supremacy, power, speed, strength and general right-of-way over everyone and everything else . . . I say if it is still intended to transport bodies then better to discard it completely. In its place let us go around in electric-driven chairs or slip on a pair of atom-powered roller skates and in a normal erect standing position go rolling along the highways. Paying $3,000 for an oversized death trap that should be available at $600, oiling it, parking it, greasing it, washing it, insuring it, polishing it, gassing it up, cleaning the inside, checking its tires, keeping it in water, keeping it in repair, keeping its accessories up to date, checking its battery, having water added, keeping a spare, keeping the spare's air pressure up, changing tires, to say nothing of keeping up the payments and renewing the licenses, both car's and driver's, appear off hand to be a frustrating way to frustrate one's life. Why not simplify things by admitting the folly of going places per se under prevailing conditions and adjust to an evoluting sensory process wherein one can mentally transport himself anywhere at any time for any purpose without so much as moving.

149

As matters stand now we have taken the living room outdoors and put wheels under it, adding in the process a super abundance of good old American gadgetry of which there just is no equivalent . . . car radios, heaters, ash trays, cigarette lighters, floor rugs, foot lights, widow wipers, television sets, et cetera. Of course all of this is just a duplication of the ease, stagnation and minimal existence of the living room, that is to say no noise, no knock, no carbon deposit, no back fire, no steering, no gear changing, no thinking, nothing but TV, radio, indigestion, decaying teeth, ulcers, more death. And the area occupied by the person dying, maimed or driving is about one two-hundredth part of the total volume of bulbous metal, glass and chrome of the car itself which is required to move in strictly limited, minimal space on roads, streets, parking lots and garages. Moreover this device to obtain the greatest possible sale must be made in the best tradition of mass pressing, chrome ribbed and decorated to meaningless and aesthetically foul decoration with hideous grills, light accessories and bumper forms both archaic and grotesque with every part devoid of function, beauty or grace. The whole is a moveable junk heap, American style, of which there is no equivalent anywhere . . . technically superior, technically low or on any plane you wish to judge it. It is a categorical fact that the taste of the American people is confined solely to their mouths. And as proof thereof look at the present crop of automobiles . . . the color, the color division areas, the side forms, the decorations in chrome, the five foot doors that cannot be fully opened, the broken up and uneven floors, the insignia spotted about the car, the gymnastics of entering and leaving, the use of materials, the total impact of snobbery, the lack of functional grace and utilitarian line, the sheer junk quality auguring breakdown, the attempts at styling old hat in six months. Only the Rolls Royce—provided the makers could be induced to knock a something or other off the radiator top—and it is a radiator, not a tooth ribbed, lip enveloped sex symbol—can be said to approach anything near the aesthetic and technical concept to which I have been alluding.

If at this point I have not wholly dispensed with the American passenger car on technical and functional grounds and grounds of intrinsic hazards, then I here now do so on aesthetic grounds alone. I suppose it is acceptable to exhibit one's deranged neurosis, disordered mind and foul taste in the privacy of one's own closet, but to do so on a public street at the risk of taking and losing life is really quite another matter.

I am reminded again of travels to cultures where inhabitants roam the world without moving, of cultures where the one imported automobile is owned by the community and cannot move until every square inch of attachable area is covered by upwards to twenty people. I am reminded, too, of so called civilized cultures where selfishness, haughty show off, overemphasized privacy, superiority, founded on the intrinsically artificial and basically unsound, on the overwhelming singleness of purpose toward personal death that defines an unexplainable factor which points to a refusal to know or do any different.

Pity, then, only yourselves in your own stew. As for me, I've left.

I was in a res-taurant in Houlton, Maine, one of these stool situations where you hang over a counter, and this man came in and sat down beside me, and I sensed this extraordinary aroma about him, his aurora and radiation effects I've been talking about, the extraordinary purity about it, and it made me curious, and it made me even more curious when he just opens up and says, well, I slept by the road last night.

And I said well, what do you mean? Well, he said, I slept by the road, I do it every night. And I said, do you have a sleeping bag or a blanket? No, no. And I said, well, could you explain this? So he gets out this piece of paper, which is 8-1/2 by 11, originally, he's had it folded so many times that its folds are now worn, and it says, I am so and so, member of Indian tribe number so and so, and my Head Chief is so and so. And this was his passport and permission to sleep in the bushes. He made it clear that he preferred that to a bed or a hotel or a motel, and it was very clear he didn't have the money, wasn't interested in it even if he did . . . and as far as I'm concerned, this odor about him was the ground . . . it was radiating all around him.

And I asked him where he was going, and he said, well, I've been down to Connecticut, and I'm on my way back to my people. And I asked him did someone pick you up, or did you hitchhike? And he said, no, we don't do that sort of thing. So I said, did you come on the expressway, on the main roads? He thought how stupid can you get. I'm an Indian, I go across the fields, through the woods. He said, we have trails. When we go from Connecticut up through to our people in New Brunswick and Nova Scotia, we go on the trail. Here he was, he was without a car, without money, and I tried to get out of him what he'd been doing in Connecticut, he didn't quite say, and I asked him did he have a wife, was he returning home, and he wouldn't say that either. He made it very clear that he slept by the trail, and there was a trail from Connecticut to Eastern New Brunswick.

Every question I asked just made me appear more stupid, it was his natural way of going. When I go from Connecticut to Maine I'm stupid, I go by train, or bus, or car, horse and buggy, motorcycle, bicycle, on the road. And he in effect said how stupid are you? Why don't you use the trail?

I

Summering Fall light-like seemed
unheavy as the dark with spots that let in ether but stopped
alpha radiation cold
    bright entrails of
    To the East the islands whose fragile shores encrus-
tations weighed amber green
    Seeking horizons languid pale
    I grieved without grief neither knowing tears nor
that she had gone though the recollections of this sorrow
stayed restayed never went away
    Is still here
    Presses upon me
    Makes has made me envious of those with sisters
    Marion
    Marion
    That I might be more full enriched be less ego-
centric more relatable considerate kind
    Because of her
    Because of her her passing my staying she gone me
in the ravines of solitude the depths at the bottom with
antagonisms depressions moody glooms non talkative
stupid even cruel

II

But more significantly
More particularly unable to adjust to or so much as use
The telephone whose voices babbled me
The radio whose waves carried more of the same
The television whose eye seemed crossed
The electricity whose gadgetry confounds me
The automobile whose gears never mesh
The airplane whose wings don't flap
All these all of everything non organic
Not of the family of nature
Were no part of me or mine
For I rejected them
Needing only the sky to cover me
The water to quench me
The fire to warm me
The earth to sustain me
Blessed blessed was I among all the many

III

In this simple state
With only the memory of her gone
I pursued my days
Till the memory thinned
And midst this admixture
Of adversity repulsion
Revision I uttered
The hope that my peoples
My tribes of people would could
Finally find their inherited **way**

I'm a physicist. In physics, I look at you and you are a plasma. A plasma is an invisible, gaseous-like, jello-like something which is living. In this act of living you are radiating an energy, you are receiving an energy, you are expanding, you are contracting, you are living, you are dying, you are glowing, you are not glowing. This is a tremendous simultaneous action. And this is within your skeleton, and if you talk to a minister he calls it your soul, and if you talk to me it's a plasma. And this plasma has many, many faculties which are undeveloped.

In our system we say I have senses, I can see, I can hear, I can feel, but I contend that our culture has so dimmed them, and bruised and banged them, that a person in 24 hours, using all five, does it for less than two minutes, just a few seconds and it would be an extraordinary person, indeed, who would use five. Most people use maybe three, maybe two.

So as you sit there, your plasma, which has your name on it, is transmitting on a frequency which has a number, and I, sitting here, knowing that number, I can, in effect, tune my system to the same number, and I can reach you without speaking to you, without writing to you, without using a phone.

Now this number, which is your frequency, which is your plasma, in addition to speaking to me without words about symbols and about business, can transmit to me some values which I could pass on to others, but these others must be on the same frequency. So it ends up that you are going through an orbit, and you are alone with it, and I have come in here on my orbit, and I'm leading you for a few minutes right here. My orbit is crossing yours at this point while we're sitting here, and it's up to me in these few minutes that we're together to determine what your frequency is. Now it's possible that you and I could continue through space and time, I might meet you again at some crossing of our orbits, but in general, in general, your orbit is either above mine, or below mine, or off phase, or at right angles, and in the physics of the situation it's quite improbable that I could determine your number easily.

In our orbits, where mine has crossed yours, it is possible that I could reorient my orbit through my own power of adjustment, my own plasma, so that I could, at this moment of corresponding with you my orbit would be the same as yours, my radiation would be the same as yours. My problem is: are these things that you are radiating to others, are they to your knowledge the best that you've got, are they positive, negative?

What I want to say is that this plasma has been given you to express, to fulfill, to civilize, and you are charged with the responsibility of letting it survive, letting it develop. And to use it well. And the educational system, the church and the government, the newspapers have bruised, mutilated, damaged, upset and disturbed this. And now, knowing this, what can you do to revive this juice in you, and what aids are there, and the sad part is there are no aids of any kind, no textbooks you can read or systems you can espouse or parties you can join, this is a personal thing. Your plasma has your name and it's up to you to fulfill your name. And however you may feel, doubt or question whether you're negative or positive, you must believe in yourself. I have this, it is mine, it was given to me, I believe in it, however many flaws, however many errors, however many wrong decisions, however many negatives, I have this, I am positive about it. I will radiate it and if there's someone who receives, fine, they are radiating, let us hope that their radiation corresponds with mine momentarily.

One Is
A Plasma
Of Energy

158

Belfast, ME.
1980

One is a plasma of energy.
Simultaneously living, dying, oscillating, passive/
expanding, contracting/sending, receiving/
alert, dead/seeing, blind/hearing, deaf/breathing,
exhaling.
A four dimensional space form of height, length, breath,
time.

Proceeding, returning with such speed in an orbital
arc of such magnitude that the path is a straight line.

And at such a speed there is no past, present or
future.

Only a NOW of/for fulfillness, all or nothing.

The plasma is/was forever present, here
from the beginning of the beginning.

Created, set up by natural formulation and design.

It will always be, never die, cease, extinguish
or reduce in strength.

Its characteristics were instantly and
permanently formed at one's inception, never to
be altered in any way by parents, schools, churches,
experiences or events.

It is

Nine to ten months later is was given your name

It is you, yours

And all the knowledge, experience you have, had.
Will experience.

Its container is your physical body which at
death will drop away while your plasma will continue in
orbit through space at speeds of no present no
future.

You will always **be.**

Ours

This once primeval terrain
Indelibly signatured
With my hoofs
And those of my kind
Post glacial
Pre and post Abnaki
Kind friends of the dawn
Who succored us
We them in mutual regard
Withstood the road cutters
The timber barons
The legislators
Their changing rules
The governors
Curtis
Longley
Et al al
The acid rains
The industrial pollution
The radioactive ash
The geologists
The mad gunners
Of MASS., CONN.
Unfriendly ME.
We're here
Been here a long time
Longer than you
Better adjusted than you
More certain
Less afraid
Not bound up
With tensions
& griefs and
Sorrows to no end.
Leave us
Leave us **be**

M e

Joy glows where confusion was
In rills of light a beam
So near the day
So far the song
To night: greeting.

Finding souls I find my own
Embracing ideas I know mine
Loving you I love me
Hating them I hate myself
Hurting killing I murder I
Self-erasing I become me.

I scuttle existences
Dynamite memory, ridding dross by fire
I recast progression's tangent
Seek the Neanderthal line
Glean by moon's wish doing.

I renew renewal
And get out.

No more the distant hope
(Who hopes, died)
This here is it
I am the one
What follows is **next.**

Prayer

161

Belfast, ME,
1978

Oh lake, plain of waters
    surround me
    flow through me
    press upon me
    wash my spirit

Oh lake, sheet of waters
    cover me
    smother my limbs
    submerge all of me
    bathe my body

Oh lake, layer of waters
    water of the deep vale
    give my people strength
    moisten our eyes
    refresh our children

Oh lake of water
    sustain us
    through to the end of the **years**

Acknowledgements

This book was compiled from the personal files of Bern Porter, and the Bern Porter collections at the following libraries: Maine State Library, Augusta, Maine; Longfellow Library, Bowdoin College, Brunswick, Maine; and Miller Library, Colby College, Waterville, Maine. The editor thanks the librarians in charge of those collections (Patty Bouchard, Augusta; Diane Gutcher, Bowdoin; and P. A. Lenk, Colby) for their generous assistance.

Previous publishing history, when known, of the writings in this book is listed below, following the page number where it appears. If published for the first time here, the source of the original typescript or holograph (BP=Bern Porter's personal files; MSL=Maine State Library; BC=Bowdoin College; MLCC=Miller Library at Colby College) is listed.

1—Do Something!
The Packages (3): Holograph, MLCC.
Clothes (4): Chapter 2 of *I've Left*, Something Else Press, New York, 1971.
Doldrums (9): Appeared as a pamphlet, illustrated by Porter, under the title, *Doldrums: A Study in Surrealism*, A.I. Press, Newark, New Jersey, 1941.
The Westfield (12): Holograph, MLCC.
Listen Up (13): Letter to the Editor, *Waldo Independent*, Belfast, Maine, April 9, 1987.
Jesus Wants Me For A Sunbeam (16): Holograph, MLCC.
How Many Sons Do You Have ? (18): Holograph, MLCC.
The Cold Fish Saga (20): Typescript, BP.
Song Titles (21): Typescript, BP.
Barbara's Belfast (22): Holograph, MLCC.
QE2 (25): Typescript, BP.
Waterfight (26): Appeared as a pamphlet, illustrated by Porter, under the title, *Waterfight*. First edition, A.I. Press, Newark, New Jersey, 1941; second edition, L.A. Press, Washington, D.C., 1941.
Not At All: A Psalm Written In Tumultuous Days (29): Published in *Leaves Fall*, Vol. 1, No. 2, Bluffton, Ohio, November, 1942.

2—Sing That Meat
Song (32): Typescript, BP.
Sestina Modi (34): Published in *Vision*, Wiscasset, Maine, Vol. 3, No. 4, 1981.
All Over The Place (35): Published in *Circle*, No. 4, Berkeley, California, 1945.
Blank Verse (41): Typescript, BP.
Statement (42): Holograph, MLCC.
Found Story (44): Published in Porter's *Art Productions, 1928-1965*, Marathon Press, Pasadena, California, 1965.
How It Works In ABC Form (45): Published in *West Coast Poetry Review*, Issue 19, Vol. 5, No. 3, Reno, Nevada.
Sonnet For An Elizabethan Virgin (47): Typescript, BP.
Unseeing Eyes (48): Published in *Leaves Fall*, Vol. 1, No. 4, January 1943, Bluffton, Ohio.
Black. White. (50): Published in Porter's *Gee-Whizzels*, Bern Porter Books, Belfast, Maine, 1977.
Guide To Found Arts (51): From an interview with George Myers, Jr., in *Puckerbrush Review*, Vol. 5, No. 1, Orono, Maine, 1982.
Towns Of The North (53): Typescript, BP.
A Dialectic For Vibrations And Non-Vibrations (54): Typescript, BP.
Two-Name Towns Of The North (55): Typescript, BP.
Many Have Heard Words (56): Typescript, BP.
The Card Index Song For The Filing Sisters (57): Published as a broadside as part of *Crossed Wires*, South Solon Press, Solon, Maine, 1978.
Sciart Manifesto (58): Excerpt from Porter's *Physics for Tomorrow*, privately published, Tasmania, 1959.
Plot (60): Typescript, BP.
Sources Of Creation (62): Published in *Vision*, Vol. 1, No. 3, Wiscasset, Maine, 1978.
Myrtle Beach Before And After The Storm (65): Published as postcard in *Word Art*, The Maine Festival, Brunswick, Maine, 1982.
Far, Far Away And Out In Front So Very Much So (66): Published in *The Maine Poets Festival Book 1979*, The Dog Ear Press, Bar Harbor, Maine, 1979.
The Last Acts of Saint Fuckyou (67): Privately published as a broadside by Porter, 1975, and as a book by Xexox Sutra, Madison, Wisconsin, 1985.

3—Notes From A Life In Publishing
My Origins As A Book Artist (74): Excerpt from an interview in *Umbrella*, Glen-

The text and cover of *Sounds That Arouse Me* were designed on Crummet Mountain by Edith Allard.

Editorial and Production Assistance: Angela Colwell, Devon Phillips, Carol Fritzson, and Kelly Beekman

Tilbury House staff: Mark Melnicove, Eric Rector, Jolene Collins, and Robert L. Johnston

Imagesetting: High Resolution, Inc., Camden, Maine

Printing (covers): Western Maine Graphics, Norway, Maine

Printing (text) and Binding: BookCrafters, Chelsea, Michigan

In addition to the trade paper and cloth editions, *Sounds That Arouse Me* has been bound in slipcases individually decorated by Bern Porter in a limited edition of twenty-six copies (designated A-Z), numbered and signed by the author. In addition, each slipcase contains an original, signed typescript or holograph by Bern Porter.

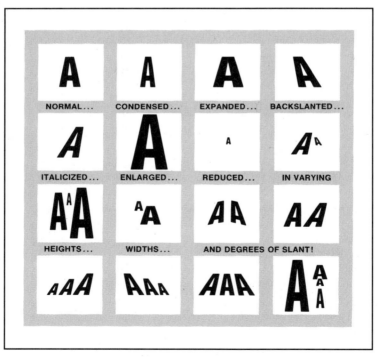

Found poem by Bern Porter